GOING TO MÉXICO

Stories of My Peace Corps Service

To Lisa,
A real asset
to CCL,
Best Wishes
Dave

David H. Greegor | 2/18/17

Peace Corps Volunteer, México
2007-2011

To Sonya, Cary, Tessa
and my friends in México

Contents

INTRODUCTION

When my wife, Sonya, and I left the Peace Corps México program in 2011, after having volunteered for over three years, I mentioned that I might combine the stories I'd been casually writing about some of our wonderful experiences into a book. "Do you mean you'd write a *real* book?" she questioned. "Yeah, right, I guess," I replied. "If I paste the stories together it should make a book or at least a comic book" (I believe very weak humor to be my main writing strength). She threw back her head, "Ha, you've been threatening to write a book about various topics since we were nuptially tethered back in the Pleistocene, to win a Pulitzer, and to buy me a ragtop BMW, a 22-year old Chippendale dancer, and a pedigree labradoodle. Look at me, I'm still sharing a '96 Toyota 2-wheel drive beater pickup with you; I'm still married to *you*; and our dog is a 17 year old arthritic and crazed half-labrador." Sonya did not really say this, of course, because she is a kind, compassionate, and *very* patient person, and she has been a huge help with this book project. I could not be more serious – for once.

Unfortunately, had she said it or even thought it, she would have been right. No ragtop, no hunk husband, no labradoodle. Why not? Well, I have several weak, very personal reasons which I will share:

Autobio insight 1: defective brain. I have loved writing, and for years have written emails, Facebook messages, and notes on toilet stall walls, but with no resultant income increase. I've also kept personal journals since I was a teen, written newspaper and magazine editorials, and scientific journal articles. But, this is my first book, which should make enough money to put me in the one percent bracket – the upper, not the lower. Oh, I have written entire book outlines and even a chapter or two scribbled on a bedside notepad during episodic 3 a.m. brainstorms. Brainstorms, at least mine, seem to be "storms" that originate in some mystery organ of my body other than the brain, let's say for sake of discussion, the pancreas, an organ not reputed to house any rationale thinking cells. Why do I say this? Because the result of these pancreatic storms is so often downright preposterous when illuminated by the light of the next day, it ends up in the wastebasket. *Going to México* never made it to the security of the wastebasket, even though it begged to be put out of its misery many times.

<u>Autobio insight 2</u>: lack of talent. For example, take the James boys, Patterson and Michener. They would have guffawed at my assignment and written my book while relaxing on a hotel toilet or maybe while waiting for their bottle of *Chivas Regal* at Delmonico's. Not a decade.

<u>Autobio insight 3</u>: procrastination/dedication. I have heard many famous authors say that to become as famous as they are (their chest detonates at that point) one has to be able to sit down at the computer in the eye of a hurricane at 8 a.m., take a break and a shot of scotch at 10 a.m. and return to the keyboard until noon, all while the hurricane is buffeting a screaming baby who is going unfed with its diaper exploding. At noon, the famous author would eat a watercress sandwich washed down with bourbon, feed and change the damned baby and be back to the keyboard from 1 to 5 with intermittent shots of whatever was in the cabinet. Famous authors don't relate to my whining cries of procrastination, like, "Ye gads, my little toe is so sore, maybe I'll go to the ER and write that two page introduction sometime next month." Or, "Oops, I can't miss the last installment of *As the World Turns* but that story needs a better title. Later, alligator." Or, "Hmmmm… maybe I'll think about that weird margin next Tuesday."

Autobio insight 4: generalizations. I over-generalize and always have which generates at the very least a mild rebuff from Sonya. For example, I might say, "Most, if not all, Mexicans love gaudy colors." In essence I did say almost exactly that. Well, did I take a survey or a poll before making that statement? No. I just assumed that since everything is so colorful in México, even toilet paper (maybe not), that the vast majority are addicted to color. If not to color, my next assumption would be that they are addicted to LSD and in a hallucinogenic state – all the time. What's wrong with that reasoning? Aren't those fair generalizations? Absolutely.

Hopefully these stories in *Going to Mexico* convey that Sonya and I truly loved our Peace Corps experience and living in México. I have, however, found it a challenge to explain in words the synergistic effect México and the Peace Corps had on me. The reader should know that we weren't just out of college like so many Peace Corps volunteers are; we were retired and spry candidates for Happy Geezer Acres Retirement Community. The chemistry of the Peace Corps and México and the timing of the diversion in our lives was "just right," as Goldilocks discovered.

Certainly another objective of this book is to convey the pure goodness we found in the Peace Corps endeavor and the Mexican people. Too much news today about México is terrifying, but the drug cartels are not what México is about. They certainly have their impacts in regards to corruption, distrust of the government and the police, and real danger in certain areas, but the people do not seem to let it overwhelm them.

Going to México is a collection of independent and near-chronological stories which I began writing in early 2008, within a few months of completing our three month Peace Corps language and culture training. The last story, *La Casita*, was written several days after returning to the United States Essentially, *Going to México* is a three year memoir.

We loved all of those twenty or so communities where our projects took us, but one community seemed to emerge above the rest: Chitejé de Garabato. Garabato is featured in the story, *Falling from Grace in Garabato*. The people of that tiny community embraced us without hesitation on our very first official work day and continued until our very last work day, more than three years later. I don't mean that we stayed in their embrace for three years!

In each of these ten stories, I have attempted to allude to some facet of the innate genuineness of Mexicans and to the humorous side of my personal experiences. To find both was easy.

It was on a Seattle summer day, after we had returned to the United States, I was picking up my now five year old grandson at his day care, and I had just unbuckled him from his rear car seat, when he leaped into the driver's seat, grabbed the steering wheel and proceeded to twist it back and forth making motor sounds. "What are you doing, Garrett?" I asked. He shouted, "I'm going to México." I hadn't said a thing to him about México or maybe he just wanted to escape his nap, but it became a fitting title for this collection which will hopefully give the reader a glimpse of the magic of México. I remember very vividly one night walking to downtown Querétaro from our tiny casita, and Sonya saying, "We probably will never have life this good again." And, even though I had been working all day in a small village and was beat, I could only agree with her. And, I still do.

David H. Greegor
Spring, 2017

You Can Smoke Ever'where

Zihuatenejo, México. New Year's Day 2010.

"One of the many ffings I love about México (hic, belch....) is that ever'one still smokes EVER'WHERE!" It was 6 a.m. To this seriously inebriated gringo* who had just emerged from an all-night bar draped over an equally soused female companion, the lip of the curb must have seemed like the rim of the Grand Canyon. (*gringo = norteamericano; some are offended by the term gringo, but you have to admit, it is crisp and universal). Both were teetering precariously as they contemplated their options: to jump or not to jump. Their audience was small at that hour on New Year's Day. Me. After staring into the chasm for what seemed like an eternity, he slowly lifted his gaze to look past me and down the street toward his hotel. Our hotel. I had seen him several times before perched across from the hotel on an open air bar stool, long before beer-thirty. According to my wife, Sonya, generalizing is one of my countless flaws and I generalized that he was a seasoned boozer: blue veins throbbing on a red face and a

7

bulbous, pocked snooper, with glazed, looking-past-you-at-the-*Pacifico*-beer-girl-on-the-wall eyes.

Sonya and I were near the end of our Christmas holiday in our favorite west coast tourist/fishing town: Zihautenejo. Zihua, as savvy gringos call it, was as close to authentic coastal México as you could expect to get accessible by pavement. Just up the road was Ixtapa, about as far as you could get from real coastal México with big chain hotels lined up on a homogeneously straight sandy beach, like Cancun, designed for Americans, Canadians and Europeans who really don't appear to be there to get to know the "real" México. Furthermore, wealthy Mexicans are reputed to enjoy Ixtapa, but they already know México.

Zihua John, we'll call him, actually sounded like he was bragging that he could come to México and smoke freely. Maybe back in the States or Canada he was accustomed to being banished to a freezing, windy alley huddled with his fellow coffin-nailers pretending to enjoy their one workday pleasure. By comparison, México is like any other developing country where many don't bother with seat belts (often because they have been removed or they're buried in the recesses of a really grungy seat) and where it's acceptable to blow smoke rings into a baby stroller (the latter part of this statement might be modestly exaggerated). I never actually saw anyone blow directly into a baby stroller, but you get the idea. But, like Zihua John said, "You can smoke ever'where."

I love México but my love of México has nothing to do with the freedom of smoking everywhere or living on the wild side, unencumbered by the inconvenience of seat belts or being forced to smoke in a gusty alley. My passion for México runs deeper than that and developed slowly over five decades. By the time we spent that Christmas in Zihua, Sonya and I had been living in México just over three years as Peace Corps volunteers, but our love affair really began when we lived in Tucson in the early 1970s and made forays into Sonora, often only as far as Nogales for dinner and a tequila bender (we were University of Arizona students). It was then we began the slow process of falling in love with México.

I'm not alone in my infatuation; we Americans love México, but why? I think much of it has to do with the fact that our cultures are so dramatically different. Allow me to make a few comparisons between the people and lifestyles of the two countries to partially prove this. For a start, Mexicans are fun and love to *have* fun. They give all appearances, true or not, of loving life and letting it unfold itself as the day or the week or the year progresses. In my drastically limited observations, there doesn't seem to be the obvious life plan or goal obsession that we Americans tend to possess. Life doesn't seem to be measured by success and failure. Their public glass always appears half full. Notice I said "public." Privately, it may be a totally different story but much of the time, I don't think so. I believe, generally speaking, the good-natured, fun-loving Mexican in public is truly a good-natured and fun-loving individual. Being able to smoke unconditionally is just one aspect of that "fun face" that encompasses laughter, tequila, cigarettes, endless jokes, karaoke crooning – all a huge part of Mexican life. Mexicans can conjure up one zillion reasons for a party, and time and place are never obstacles. Whether in a beach town, a poor inland village, or a Mexican migrant worker gathering in the United States, Mexicans, unlike us starched gringos, are hardwired for partying. Combine that with warm, clear sea water and you have a good explanation for why we flock to México on holidays. We crave that ability to cut loose on a moment's notice.

I think we are intrigued by the fact that Mexicans don't worry too much about being on time. I once played a coffee house gig with a small blues band who initially told me that we didn't need to practice together. I finally talked them in to it so the leader set the practice for 5 p.m. I showed up punctually at 5. The last member, the female singer, straggled in at 7. They were all members of a larger jazz band which they told me started practice at 7:30; the additional members of that band started drifting in around 8. Our gig was the next night, and it went fine.

Take a slice of life at 5 a.m. in the two countries, for example. In the United States, we're driving to the gym to keep our bodies forever twenty; in México they're hauling a rented karaoke machine in the open bed of a beat-up pickup to someone's garage to continue the wedding party until 10 a.m. or later! It has been said that there are no two countries in the world that share a border which are so radically different as the United States and México, and fun may be one of the most obvious cultural differences. In my estimation, it is not trivial.

México is a cornucopia of charisma and diversity. On most mornings in Zihua, while Sonya was still comatose in the hotel, I was on the beach before dawn, sipping bad 7-11 coffee, writing in my journal and watching several elderly women, silhouetted against a rising sun, as they painstakingly swept the beach with homemade brooms. The idyllic, almost surreal scene was ironically complemented by background salsa music pulsing out over the surf from Zihua John's all-night bar, while fishing boats quietly returned from a night of seining. I would not expect to see this scene of the beach-sweepers north of the border.

Poverty is a way of life in México and not hidden or something of which to be ashamed. But, while we have plenty of poverty in the United States we tend to try, at least, to sweep it under the carpet unless someone manages to break free by having a highly desirable talent. It doesn't fit the "American portrait" *until* they can demonstrate "rags to riches." Consequently, the poor rise out of poverty in the United States with difficulty, but it does happen. In contrast, in México, it is frequently the poor who remain poor without any overt discontent, but who contribute greatly to the folk art, music and dance that gives México such uniqueness and cultural diversity.

I admit we were initially disappointed when we were assigned to the Peace Corps México program in 2007. Even though we always had enjoyed our vacations in México, we were thinking of an assignment someplace new and exotic like Nepal, Africa, Bhutan, Thailand, or India. Regardless, we accepted. By a stroke of good fortune, our Peace Corps training took place in Querétaro, possibly the most beautiful and clean historic large city in México. By the time we finished the three month training process, we realized how myopic we had been about this country of many faces. Like most gringos, we were familiar with the coastal beaches and the border towns, but ignorant of everything in between—in other words, most of the country. Querétaro, with its beauty and history, has become the poster child of México with a burgeoning economy attracting major international companies. We had never heard of it.

Once we accepted the México invitation, I dug out the "M" volume of our glacial era World Book encyclopedia, complete with photos of grizzled old guys in sombreros straddling a mule or taking a siesta under a mango tree. Sonya, way savvier than I am, went straight to the internet. Suddenly, México became appealing. It is not only accessible, but it is culturally and biologically one of the richest countries in the world. There are twelve countries globally that possess 70% of the world's species and México is one of those twelve, in large part because of such a diversity of habitats. In addition, the Mexican government recognizes almost 70 indigenous languages, one of the highest in the world.

Even before our Peace Corps experience, I had been struck by an indefinable quality about México that seemed to transcend its diversity and beauty. For lack of a better term, I call it *magic*. Hard as it is to describe, much of the time we lived there I felt as though I were in a mini-trance. It was spiritual and mystical at the same time. It certainly had a lot to do with the people, especially the children. The great Mexican writer Carlos Fuentes was asked in an interview years ago why there was so much magic and surrealism in Latin American fiction. He answered that the great theme of novels since Cervantes and *Don Quixote* is the relation between reality and illusion, between ordinary daily life and imagination. That, I believe, describes México perfectly – a blend of ordinary and extraordinary.

México, like all developing tropical-subtropical countries, provides experiences that forcefully engage every sense. Smell is my favorite and possibly the most pronounced. Smell elicits deep feelings and mysterious inexplicable memories, and México has endless provocative and nauseating fragrances, both natural and man-made, from flowers to perfume to rotting rivers.

The wonder of México, which when combined with sensory experiences, all hammering synergistically on heart, mind, and soul created, at least at times for me, a euphoric state. México's diverse peoples, nature, weather, and even its beaten land and polluted cities, often transported me to another dimension where I felt as if I were only an observer and never a true participant, watching the unfolding of a magic show played on a constantly revolving stage where the activities and the people – virtually everything from sunrise to sunset – were never static. Planning your day was impossible and often mentally exhausting. Every day, every *single* day, was different, often dramatically different from the preceding and following days. This seems to possibly explain why Mexicans don't draft out tight daily schedules and fastidious plans, but tend to go with the flow and let life unfold itself to them.

And finally, the people. The people made the magic real. I loved our Peace Corps projects in the rural, poor communities. Without exception, the village people were always appreciative, humble, kind, gentle and fun. I would like to believe our admiration was mutual. This passion for small villages and their residents is not news to most returned Peace Corps volunteers. México, with the help of the Peace Corps, collaboratively changed us forever. While we developed deep and permanent friendships in Querétaro, where we lived, it was the people of the small communities who really burrowed deep into our hearts and took up permanent residence.

Three months after that Christmas of 2010 in Zihuatenejo, we said goodbye to México and our friends and returned to the United States. Some say that returning to the cubicled work world, cold dark nights alone with TVs embedded in monotypic silent neighborhoods can be a more difficult transition than leaving the States for sun-drenched beaches, endless fiestas and vibrant, people-clogged plazas. Let's put it this way, neither Sonya nor I have needed psychiatric help since returning, perhaps in large part attributable to that magic magnet of México, which is still every bit as strong as it was the day we left. That magic certainly transcended, for me at least, the all-night bars and being able to smoke "ever'where."

FALLING FROM GRACE IN GARABATO
-EVENING JOURNAL ENTRIES-

Wednesday, December 19, 2007.

Toma de Protesta (Swearing-in Ceremony), Peace Corps Headquarters, Querétaro, México. Today we Peace Corps trainees of Group 5 became official volunteers in the relatively new México program. The first group went through this ceremony in 2004. Exhausted from three months of intensive training, our group of twenty has been struggling a lot in the final weeks with Spanish exams and projects all coming due simultaneously. Consequently, we were swearing a lot, too, but not necessarily in preparation for the big event. It was our way of semi-quietly protesting the arduous workload.

Up to today, we had been referred to as aspirantes, or "those who aspire," a tentative status reinforced by the fact that we could have been dropped from the program at any point during the three months of training, or even later as volunteers, for that matter, depending on how heinous the crime. Take for example, the seemingly benign requirement to learn the Spanish language.

We were supposed to be speaking Spanish 24/7, but I doubt any of our bosses would have considered axing us for not speaking Spanish every waking moment. We were, however, expected to be reasonably fluent by the end of training, but most of us failed that criterion except those who already knew the language. Fluency, we discovered, was very subjectively evaluated by Peace Corps Mexico. In my case, the woman who gave me my fluency test liked my sense of humor and gave me an outlandishly high rating, even higher than Sonya's, who was close to fluent. One fable going around was that a good indicator of level of fluency was whether or not you were dreaming in Spanish. I remember having numerous dreams affiliated with México and the Mexican people, but I don't remember any words of ANY language being exchanged and certainly not dreams I care to discuss publicly.

Only the rare aspirante attempted to speak Spanish constantly, it was too exhausting. It was especially difficult for those of us who were married. Unless you have spoken Spanish for any extended period in your past, which a few in our group had, it was too exhausting to keep it going when you were out of earshot of your host family or your Spanish teachers. Later, I came to know one couple who intentionally spent their three months of training with separate host families to force them to avoid falling back on English when they were alone together. That couple was dedicated beyond normalcy. Or maybe they just wanted an excuse for a three-month break from each other. (After our intense training period, I could relate and I know Sonya could, too.) Sonya and I tried to establish a block of time each evening – I think initially 30 minutes rapidly whittled to zero – to talk only in Spanish with each other. By the end of the day we found ourselves so exhausted that we barely felt like communicating at all, in any language. Our apartment, attached to our host family's home, was two rooms – a bedroom and a sitting room – so we needed to be VERY compatible, which, fortunately, most of the time, we were. But by the end of a day starting at 8 a.m. at Olé, our Spanish language school, and ending around 5 p.m., we were shot. And almost always we still had homework to do after that.

One linguistically challenged member of our group seemingly made up his own language that was clearly not English, Spanish, Spanglish, or Texican. If anything, it sounded closer to Speaking in Tongues, a divine language unknown to the speaker. But, in this case that was doubtful because I think he knew what he was saying. It was just that no one else did. Furthermore, it tended to occur only when he was under stress, which seemed to be much of the time. One perceptive(?) aspirante suggested that it could be *Nahuatl*, the ancient language of the Aztecs, but no one, including our Spanish teachers, knew Nahuatl, and no one believed he knew Nahuatl since he clearly had trouble with both Spanish and English.

Tuesday, January 8, 2008.
Most of us were at our sites today, having begun our Peace Corps assignments. Sonya and I lucked out and got assigned to the state SEMARNAT office in Querétaro. SEMARNAT is essentially the Mexican equivalent of the Environmental Protection Agency, and we are to work as consultants on environmental issues. Today was our first day on the job. We are ecstatic with our assignment because we have come to love Querétaro.

Being dedicated anal gringos, we arrived promptly at 8 a.m., Sonya in a skirt and blazer and me in a rarely seen white shirt and tie. Most of the SEMARNAT professionals arrived about 9:15, coincidently just as the short, cute, fireball director, Patti, roared into the parking lot and sprinted to her office. Patti gave the welcoming address at the Protesta, in English; her English is flawless. She is not your typical Mexican bureaucrat. For starters, she is a she. Moreover, as we found out later, she gets things done. Her opening comments to us after she whisked us into her office, were, "You two are volunteers, not paid employees, so wear what you want and decide your own schedule. If I were you I would dress casually and arrive around 9 a.m., work until 3, go home, have your comida (main meal of the day) and take a siesta. If you are going into the field, like you will be in about five minutes, then ignore what I just said. The field work day can end anytime and sometimes very late." And then she diplomatically dismissed us. That was the last time we dressed professionally for work.

An hour later we were bouncing along a cobblestone road south of Querétaro along with our SEMARNAT guide, a young man named Jorge, and a few others to whom we had not been introduced. We were headed to three communities nestled high in a picturesque little watershed on the state line that drains south into the state of México and eventually into one of the most polluted rivers in México, the Rio Lerma. (These three impoverished communities were destined to become our favorites among many. They, above the rest, gave me that feeling of euphoria and magic with virtually every visit of which there were many). As we traveled from Chitejé de Garabato, our first stop, to El Varal, our second, and then finally on to Chitejé de la Cruz, my sense of belonging to each community grew, despite knowing no one.

Our Peace Corps contract specified that I would be advising SEMARNAT and communities on watershed environmental issues such as erosion and deforestation. Sonya's main role has something to do with environmental education, but exactly what, was vague. However, at each of the three communities, Jorge introduced us as "my good friends from the States, the outhouse specialists." We had known Jorge less than a day. This title came as a bit of a shock to Sonya and me because it felt like a demotion from watershed specialists to latrine detailers.

The people of the villages have been constructing waterless outdoor toilets as part of a sustainable community project and apparently Jorge needed experts from the formidable México neighbor to the north, the U.S. of A. We had told Jorge earlier that we built one outhouse a long time ago on our Idaho property. It didn't seem to make any difference because by day's end we were thinking we truly were outhouse experts. At Chitejé de la Cruz, after introducing us, Jorge even asked us to say a few words about our outhouse experience. In horribly distorted

Spanish I tried to make a joke out of it and said that our only real experience was that we had "Used outhouses a lot in the past." No one, including Jorge, laughed, because: a) my Spanish was lousy and they obviously hadn't a clue what I was saying, and b) even if a few understood, it was a bad joke — in any language.

Friday, June 20, 2008.

This morning, at the beginning of the central México rainy season, it was cloudy when we made our second trip to Chitejé de Garabato for a community meeting. The old SEMARNAT Dodge van in which we traveled was so crowded that one student intern was sandwiched on the floor behind the back seat, where you normally stash jackets and maybe a water bottle or two, and the front passenger seat was shared by a plumpish woman and her obese teenage daughter, who sat on her mother's lap. Had there even been a seatbelt available, it would not have fit around both of them. As I alluded to earlier, in many Mexican vehicles if you actually happen to find a seatbelt it is usually wrapped around a tire iron or buried under a seat where you absolutely do NOT want to stick your hand. Preposterous as it sounds, I've wondered whether it wasn't safer to go without the belt. But today, sitting on one of the back bench seats, I badly wanted a seatbelt because our driver, Jorge, immediately pegged the speedometer in a display of Mexican machismo. There were several attractive young women in the van and Jorge had made it very clear to me on several occasions that he was highly successful in scoring with the ladies. In my experience many other Mexican men made similar claims. The excessive speeds on the German autobahn are nothing compared to the Mexican autopista; we were passed like we were standing still at 85 mph.

Chitejé de Garabato, about one hour south of the city of Querétaro, basically rests on the border of the three states of Querétaro, Michoacán, and México (where México City is) and fairly close to two other states, Hidalgo and Guanajuato. Most of the residents of the small poor villages in that region are indigenous Otomí women, not unusual because the men leave to find work in the United States or in larger Mexican cities. Of the men too old to make the trip al Norte (to the United States), many often hang around the community drinking *pulque*, the regional agave drink of the rural poor. This leaves the responsibility of community work, both domestic and outdoor, largely to the women and children. Consequently, these women are industrious, organized, resourceful, generous, loving, cheerful, and sober – in the same skin.

Just past the county seat the pavement turned to cobblestone. These roads seemed older than they really were, and when I asked Jorge, he told me, completely straight-faced, in Spanish of course, "The Romans built them when they helped us build our aqueducts."

"What?" I said. "The Romans were never in the New World." He laughed and didn't respond. I don't think he knew what I meant by the term, New World. The cobblestone was rough, particularly at high speeds in an overloaded vehicle lacking any spring to its springs even under normal loads. And, with no seatbelts, most of us kissed the ceiling a few times. By the time we rolled into Garabato, we exploded from the van.

The Garabato community center, where the meeting was held, was bleak and barren, inside and out – like a cement gymnasium in the middle of a huge, dusty, grassless soccer field complex. Inside, rickety tables, a few ancient school desks, and a mixture of badly beaten metal and plastic Corona beer chairs were scattered around the cement floor. Patiently waiting for us were perhaps thirty adults, mostly women, a smattering of old guys in white plastic cowboy hats, some anorexic dogs skulking around the chairs hoping for a food tidbit to drop, and maybe a dozen toddlers, clinging to their mothers' legs or scooting around on the filthy floor. (As we came to discover, this was a pretty typical community center in the small rural villages of México.)

We got to work immediately, starting with nailing a huge, colorful Disney – like SEMARNAT banner of an environmentally healthy watershed – like nothing I'd ever seen in México with clear running streams, lush green forests, deep rich soil and happy villagers washing their clothes in the crystal streams. Sonya and I were really there to help and observe the process, which included educating the people about the importance of having a thriving watershed and conserving rather than squandering their resources, mainly wood, water, and soil. The audience included primarily those families accepted into a government program that would provide the materials for them to build waterless outhouses, rainwater cisterns, gray water filters and efficient wood-burning stoves.

Watersheds in the central volcanic belt of México are in a bad state and getting steadily worse. Huge erosion gullies in fragile volcanic soil look like miniature Grand Canyons. Climate change is affecting their water supply, but the deforestation and erosion problems are really no different from the rest of the developing world – too many people trying to eke out a living from the land on an income of $1-2 per day.

Erosion in the Central Volcanic Belt of México

After our presentation based on the unrealistic Disney cartoon watershed, the community brought out good, healthy food – tortillas, nopales (strips of cactus), chicken, cheese, etc. – and unhealthy drinks – Coke, pulque and tequila. Pulque and tequila are healthy enough were it not for the alcohol but Coke is a different story. México is the number one consumer per capita of *Coca Cola*, "black milk" as some call it, in the world. Pulque, like tequila, is a product of the agave plant, and is commonly drunk in rural areas where agave grows. It looks like skim milk and has an alcohol content that varies with the fermentation time. The taste, not subtle, is difficult to describe. The smell is easy to describe: ripe jockstraps or sweaty socks. I like the taste and can tolerate the smell, perhaps because of some wonderful locker room memories from high school. Most gringos and most Mexicans do not like pulque. The villagers love finding a gringo who acquires the taste. I drank it at Garabato today without hesitation. (And, as I later discovered, they brought it out for me every time we returned to that community and others.) With the feast underway I was soon balancing a plate of beans, tostadas, and black mole in one hand and a big glass of pulque in the other, headed for a place to sit. The empty chair in my sights was one of the flimsy metal folding ones. As I slid into it, one of the back legs, held in place with scotch tape, collapsed. I flipped over backwards followed by the food and pulque, all of which landed on my face and shirt.

After a few moments of total silence, the villagers were all over me, helping unravel me from the chair and scraping off chunks of food. The women were shocked and embarrassed almost to the point of tears. Sonya and my colleagues, on the other hand, laughed hysterically. Audibly relieved that I wasn't dead, some of the villagers started to laugh, nervously at first, but it gained momentum as I rose like Lazarus from the dead. I learned later that they thought their homemade pulque was responsible for my sudden demise.

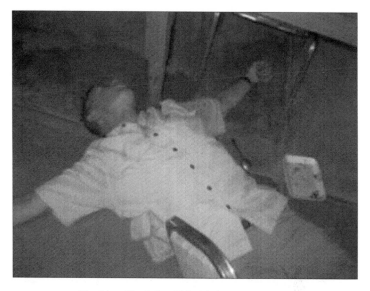

Broken Chair in Chitejé de Garabato

I filled a second plate and, this time, was escorted to a sturdier chair. Sitting next to me was a shriveled, gray-haired woman named Rosita. It is very hard to tell the age of elderly rural Mexicans because they are so weathered, but she could have been 80. Keeping with the humorous spirit, I mentioned to her that I wanted to trade her sparkling white, beautifully embroidered, blouse for my pulque and mole-stained shirt. Eyes wide and mouth open, she leaped up and said she did not feel comfortable giving me her best blouse but could get me a clean T-shirt. I tried unsuccessfully to tell her I was joking, but before I could figure out the Spanish to stop her, she

29

was out the door at a fast shuffle and headed up the hill to her tiny home. Minutes later she was back with the shirt, complete with the SEMARNAT logo plastered across the front! She wasn't even breathing hard when she carefully explained, "This is not a gift but only a loan. I can't give you my only T-shirt."

Old Rosita of Chitejé de Garabato

On our next trip to Garabato, I saw old Rosita, who was still joking with her fellow villagers about my accident. She didn't seem terribly concerned that I had forgotten to bring back what she said was her only T-shirt, but I saw her wearing another SEMARNAT shirt, one that looked newer. I think her memory of me flat on the floor covered with black mole and pulque might have seemed like a fair trade to her for the shirt, but on a later visit I returned the same shirt, cleaned, along with a brand new one

Primera Plus to Jalpan

North of the city of Querétaro and occupying 32 percent of the state of Querétaro, lies the majestic Sierra Gorda Biosphere Reserve. The Sierra Gorda is the largest biosphere reserve in México at about 950,000 acres or nearly 1,500 square miles.

Sleeping Woman in Sierra Gorda Market

It became official by Mexican presidential decree in 1997 with its primary purpose of protecting its exceptional bio- and cultural diversity. It is managed by the National Commission of Natural Protected Areas (CONANP) of the Ministry of Environment and Natural Resources (SEMARNAT), the agency where Sonya and I worked. The Sierra Gorda is the home of the phenomenally beautiful and endangered military macaws, as well as five incredible 18th century Franciscan missions designated as UNESCO World Heritage sites in 2003.

In January 2009, Sonya and I hopped a bus to *Jalpan*, the largest community in the reserve and located in the very heart of it. We had been in the Sierra Gorda on several occasions before, once during Peace Corps training for an entire week.

Our plan this time was to visit Peace Corps friends who had been personally using and promoting solar cookers (Sonya's main project), and maybe see some real wildlife, like the macaws. We were starved to see some native animal species. The environs of Querétaro, where we lived, had an abundance of livestock, such as goats, sheep, burros and cows, but of native wildlife, such as deer, raptors, peccaries, snakes, etc., we had seen very little.

Mission in the Sierra Gorda

We were told that the Sierra Gorda reserve was loaded with observable goodies. We were prepared to settle for a flea-ridden skeletal jaguar or even a worn out old featherless toucan.

I have said it before; the intercity bus system in México is one of the best in the world, maybe the best. We had been all over the country during the previous year and a half, and had yet to wrestle with a pig or a rooster for a seat. The first class buses are luxurious. One of the lines, *Primera Plus,* which serves Jalpan from Querétaro was no exception and it had been our favorite line for several reasons.

Primara Plus Intercity Bus

Reason 1: As you board the bus, the hostess hands you a *LonchiBon Sandwichón* and soft drink. This practice is relatively rare, but a handful of other bus lines do the same. The colorful bag always contains two items and is always served by an attractive young hostess in the obligatory mini-skirt and stiletto heels, who never remains on the bus to administer first aid, suppositories, an arm to support us old folks on our journey down the aisle to the bathroom or simply provide unrealistic fantasy for senior male passengers, myself, of course, excluded. In this colorful LonchiBon bag were either a Bimbo (Mexican Wonder bread, the name having nothing to do with the American derisive use of the word) bologna & cheese sandwich with one baby jalapeno slice, or a Bimbo croissant with exactly the same ingredients. And two tiny cookies. On a long trip when you haven't eaten for 24 or more hours, LonchiBons were filet mignon to the pallet. If the hostess handed one of us a croissant and the other a Bimbo sandwich, we always fought over who got the croissant because the croissant felt like it contained some fiber content.

LonchiBon!

Reason 2: The restrooms on Primera Plus buses almost, I say almost, never failed. That is not the case with buses of other companies. However, once on the three-hour trip from México City to Querétaro on Primera Plus, the toilet did fail and it was unpleasant. My nose doesn't work so well, but Sonya, who can smell a fart in France, had to bury her nose in her coat in an overheated bus, to keep from vomiting. We were in front row seats, as far as you could physically get from the restroom. The Mexicans in the back next to the malfunctioning restroom were all asleep, either unfazed or comatose from lack of oxygen.

Reason 3: Primera Plus always accepted my credencial. Credencial is short for "*credencial para la tercera edad*," the official ID for the third "age" aka senior citizens or geezers. No one ever explained to my satisfaction, and I couldn't find these Mexican age categories anywhere on the internet, but as a scientist I was determined to quantify the classification, right or wrong. So, I figured 0-30 must be the *primera edad*; 30-60 the *segunda edad*; and 60 to death, *tercera edad*. Why not get some benefits when you have reached the age when everything is pretty much going downhill? In México, it is definitely worth getting the card even if you have to do a little shufflin', mumblin', droolin' and cupping your ear when you apply.

Those of us with our credencials were entitled to some great discounts, including 50% off the cost of bus tickets and free admission to museums, ruins, galleries, etc. Even the Querétaro city buses gave us a ride for three pesos (about 21 cents) instead of five. Occasionally, but rarely, some young whippersnapper city driver gave me a nasty stare and wouldn't honor it. I guess I needed to look like I survived the Pleistocene.

The other bus line that serves Jalpan, *Flecha Amarilla* (Yellow Arrow), was second class, definitely cheaper, and also ran more frequently. However, Flecha Amarilla buses don't have bathrooms, AC, or windows that always open, and on an overnight trip they may show old *Terminator* or *Rambo* movies continuously all night. Furthermore, and maybe most importantly, they don't serve LonchiBons. Perhaps a more sobering and critical factor is that Flecha Amarilla had been known to miss an occasional curve on the road to Jalpan and go airborne.

During the peak of the summer heat, before our trip to Jalpan, we had taken Flecha Amarilla on the last bus of the day from Bernal, a popular tourist town about an hour away from Querétaro. Flecha Amarilla was the only line servicing Bernal and the last bus back to Querétaro was around 6 p.m. The driver, in an effort not to disappoint anyone and leave them stranded overnight in Bernal, packed the bus to the point that he had someone sitting on his lap, while Sonya and I sacrificed seats, allowing ourselves to be sandwiched in the aisle. Given the crowding, coupled with the heat, no bathroom, no AC, and no air circulation because the windows didn't open, I felt light-headed on carbon dioxide and armpit fumes, and started thinking that sliding off the mountain might be a preferred option.

Back to the trip to Jalpan. We snatched our LonchiBons and drink and hopped aboard, all set for a four-hour scenic ride into the beautiful Sierra Gorda mountains. We had reserved front row seats because, as everyone knows, the front is always better than the rear when driving through mountains. The first third of the trip is through farmland, flat and boring. When we hit the mountains the road did what mountain roads always do, switchback and climb. I heard that the Querétaro to Jalpan route holds the world record for curves per mile. In all, I think there are several hundred. At first, we climbed through a beautiful cactus desert almost until we reached Puerta del Cielo pass, or "door to the sky," and often, at that point, into clouds and rain. But well before we reached the pass, we knew it was not going to be another luxurious, snoozy, scenic Primera Plus bus ride. The driver must not have believed in the laws of the universe and that they tend to affect vehicles differently on sinuous mountain roads than they do on freeways... particularly vehicles of large mass, like buses. It was as if he were facing a personal challenge of either taking the most direct route through the mountains or seeing if he could do the trip using only the accelerator. When he was forced to use the brakes, he squashed them as one would a juicy cockroach.

By the time we reached the pass, Sonya had lost interest in the countryside and was focused on avoiding re-chewing her croissant sandwich she'd won in the bet. Her face was gray, her eyes sunken. Several times she said she had thought about bringing Dramamine but dismissed the idea because we were taking Primera Plus with the safest, most tranquil drivers in the world. A very young Mexican mother with a swaddled babe seated behind us was trying to discreetly cover up her dry heaves. Somewhere on the downhill slide into Jalpan, equally sinuous as the climb, my bladder so needed relief that I decided to chance the journey to the restroom. Remember, I said that we had front row seats which made the journey to the rear of the bus appear as if I was at Base Camp and staring up at Everest. I strongly considered wetting myself as a distinct alternative. Also, I was beside the window which meant I had to reach slowly and carefully across Sonya to steady myself on the aisle armrest. As I lifted my butt from the seat to make my move, the bus lurched to the right and I was instantly launched to the left, across the aisle, slamming hard against the far window, and dropping into the lap of a sleeping woman. She barely moved from her slumber, and I wasn't so sure I *could* move. If the window had been regular glass, it would have shattered, sucking me into the canyon far below. Sort of like what happens to Agent *007* every five minutes, except that I would have died from fear long before reaching the bottom, whereas Bond would have picked himself up, stared momentarily at his compound broken wrist, brushed off a few leaves, readjusted his bow tie and scaled the vertical glass-smooth granite face, using only his broken arm. In his good hand he would be clutching a wild rose he'd picked at the bottom of the canyon for his date with Dame Higgenbottom that night. When I recovered, my wrist wasn't broken or even sore so I did manage to make it back to the toilet, progressing cautiously with both hands, creeping from armrest to armrest.

No sane person ever sits on a public toilet seat in México, so when I peed, because of the continuously swerving bus I needed both hands free to keep from slamming my head into the wall. Consequently, my monster Johnson was like a fire hose out of control, and the urine stream hit everything but its intended target, the toilet bowl – sink, walls, even the mirror. Agent 007 would not have missed his target.

Coming back down the aisle, I couldn't help but notice the face of the little mama in the seat behind us. It was the color of a lime, but the baby was sleeping soundly. Sonya was literally shaking and mumbling incoherently about how she badly wanted to die. A bold statement for someone who had experienced almost sixty summers of life and was from a family of stoics, all of whom felt that revealing a visit to the doctor's office was akin to admitting you liked child pornography.

As we came into Jalpan we hit a straight stretch that Sonya told me later saved her, and probably me, from a LonchiBon launch. We pulled into the station in three hours, exactly one hour ahead of schedule. That had to be a permanent record because no bus driver could possibly beat that time and keep his bus on the road.

As Sonya shakily got to her feet, she reached down to pick up her daypack, but it was gone. She thought it had rolled backward under the seats. So, obediently, I got down on my hands and knees to look, starting below little mama's quickly vacated seat, where it was dark and smelly. And then my hand slid through something that didn't feel like bus carpeting is supposed to feel. It felt slimy. No, no, No, NO! PLEASE, NO! Chunks of Bimbo and bologna. NO, NO, NO. NOT… LonchiBons!

Author and Wife at Chuveje Falls in the Sierra Gorda

Sonya's pack? Oh, I finally found the pack across the aisle where the comatose sleeper onto whose lap I had landed, had been. This made reasonable physical sense. The pack wound up there for the same reason I had; we had been swerving *back and forth* and not pitching *forward and backward*. Had the driver used his brakes, we would have been treated to both motions.

As we walked past the driver I thought about decapitating him with my little two-inch red Swiss Army pocket knife, which I carried for just such purposes. But instead, I muttered *muchas gracias* between clenched teeth. I'm fairly certain he got the message. Our Peace Corps friends were there to pick us up, and we had a great weekend together. And the return to Querétaro? *No problema.* The new driver wasn't on a testosterone drip and Sonya was overdosed on Dramamine from our friends' stash. I could tell because she treated me really sweetly and slurred her words. The one downside? No LonchiBons.

PUEBLO MOMENTS

Thousands of sunburnt pueblos dot the Mexican landscape, and as best I know, the majority of them are poor. I was unable to visit them all. Those in which not all residents lived at the extreme poverty level would have had a famous tourist attraction or industry – such as silver, opals or a historically famous mission. We visited two renowned opal communities and found that families directly involved with the opal business lived comfortably, but their comfort did not appear to trickle very far. Many residents of these poor communities live on a few dollars a day – thus the justification for classifying México as a developing country. In the course of implementing our projects we got to know twenty or so pueblos well enough to make some general observations. Several of those, such as Chitejé de la Cruz and Chitejé de Garabato, we visited regularly and got well-acquainted with the *campesinos* (peasants) who lived there.

All of these pueblos had common characteristics, but each had its own uniqueness. A few of the common features included a very old, usually very simple, but immaculate church, a community center, several tiny house-front stores, a school or two, rudimentary cement homes, dusty, dirt streets and lots of mangy, emaciated dogs. The inhabitants were predominantly women and children and a few men, who, if present, were usually old (or looked old) and happily devoted to *pulque* and tequila. Most of the younger males worked in the cities or headed north to the States. The women were the backbone and leaders of the communities. The children, as well as the adults usually appeared pretty healthy because, as a general rule, they ate well. Actually, the rural diet was quite healthy. The downside to their diet was their beverages of choice: pulque and Coke.

We had numerous daily (one unexpected overnight in a campesino home) experiences in these pueblos that, linked together, could provide a decent picture of typical rural Mexican life. A complete portrait, however, would necessitate living in one of the communities for at least a year. I regret we didn't, but that wasn't our Peace Corps assignment – to live in a small pueblo. Even so, we came away with strong impressions and many unforgettable moments, of which I have selected a few to share. The rest I have forgotten because I didn't write them down or slept through them.

THE GRINGO WHO LIKED PULQUE

I begin this Pueblo Moment with a critical background lesson in biology. The blue agave (*Agave tequilana* or *Agave azul*) is well-known for tequila. Another popular drink, mezcal (or mescal), is made from a closely related agave, *Agave americana*. Each is officially produced only in the Mexican states of Jalisco and Oaxaca respectively. Two other drinks also come from the agave: *aguamiel*, or honey water, and pulque. Both are very popular in the small communities where we worked. Aguamiel is a non-alcoholic drink. Pulque definitely is *not* non-alcoholic.

Mexicans call the agave plant *maguey* (pronounced *ma-gay*). In the production of aguamiel and pulque, when the maguey is mature (10 to 15 years), the giant asparagus-like stalk that holds the flower is whacked off at the base. What remains are the sharp, stiff leaves and the center, or heart, which is scooped out with a big, hand-carved wooden spoon, leaving a bowl. The aguamiel – the sugary sap – drips out of the cut leaves and into that bowl and then is typically sucked out using a hollowed out gourd. I've been told a single plant can produce up to eight liters of aguamiel per day and can continue to do so for as long as six months, until it finally dies. If the aguamiel sits for a few days in the plant, it ferments into pulque – a thick, foamy, translucent white liquid, with usually 4-6% alcohol content. Pulque has a taste and stench reminiscent, to me, of body odor and ripe jockstraps. Try not to think about it, especially if you want to try pulque.

Blue Agave Plantation in Jalisco

Pulque is a taste acquired by a minority of Mexicans, usually campesinos or cheap gringos who may also be alcoholics (I don't take that personally). Apparently, it used to be more popular in the cities, but if you find it in the city, it usually is fruit-flavored to cover the true taste and smell. Even then, I don't think one would consider it a Mexican designer drink.

I first experienced pulque on a visit to Chitejé de Garabato, after helping with a SEMARNAT workshop. To get to the pulqueria in Garabato we had to cross a raw, sunbaked-to-cement soccer field only to find an unexceptional concrete building with benches outside occupied by toothless men, either slumped over and snoring or glassy-eyed and mumbling to themselves incoherently. These men were not necessarily elderly, but may have only appeared old, and they may have represented the entire adult male resident population of Garabato. No women; they were too busy managing the pueblo and their families.

This time, we drank in style from glass mugs, but normally the more traditional container is a plastic soda bottle. The odor and taste slammed my senses, but I liked the zingy, yeasty flavor of the frothy brew, immediately. And, I liked the buzz.

In less than a week the word had spread throughout the basin about the gringo who liked pulque, and the nearby communities produced some every time I visited. It didn't make any difference what we were doing, the pulque would always appear at some point, brought by the women and children, of course – especially if we were outside sweating, as if they were delivering iced tea to their fellas reaping the wheat (just like in the good old USA). Some of the women drank it, but Sonya did not, would not, but she always was polite about it.

The Author on Erosion Wall, Chitejé de la Cruz

On one occasion in Garabato, while I was helping build a rock wall on an eroded hillside, I jokingly asked the woman working closest to me, "Where's the pulque?" I had tried this trick before when I'd gotten shaky and needed a break, and almost invariably they would start giggling and someone would take off at a fast shuffle to return with three liter Coke bottles, sometimes washed, sometimes not, of the murky brew. This time, when the pulque arrived, I took a break and admired a sight one would never see in the States: a hillside covered with several generations of chattering people, moving boulders without the aid of gloves or crowbars or Superman. This included everything from barefoot infants in soiled diapers (they didn't help with the boulders; they just toddled around and smelled) to toothless women in woolen shawls and one very pregnant teenager. On that particular day, however, the slope stopped moving long enough to watch the gringo slake his thirst and calm his jangled nerves with Garabato's finest.

FALLING FROM GRACE ... REGULARLY

Not infrequently, during our time in México, when I was in an audience listening attentively, I would fall asleep. Not a doze, but a snuffle-snoring, head-flopping sleep. Almost always after comida (lunch, the big meal of the day). México is a warm country, and there is not a lot of air conditioning, even in the city of Querétaro. On one occasion, during a talk about the pine bark beetle invasion in the Sierra Gorda, given by the gentleman in the photo, and just after I had introduced him, I tilted my chair against the wall in the front row and promptly fell asleep. I woke up as the thin metal chair was collapsing under me with a resounding crash. This was at a pueblo workshop that I had organized.

These involuntary naps became a daily habit for me throughout our three months of Peace Corps training, almost always after the late afternoon comida and during a training class. When it happened, my fellow volunteers would jab Sonya, but usually she already knew and was ignoring me. On one occasion I awoke to find an anonymous message written on my note pad. A fellow volunteer, also elderly, slept through many a talk, but he had the ability to do so standing up or sitting erect.

The Author Meditating During Pine Bark Beetle Training Class in the Sierra Gorda

At least I never experienced (as best I know) what happened years ago during an exceedingly soporific presentation at a professional meeting I was attending with a close friend. The room was uncomfortably warm. A guy several rows behind me relaxed a little too much in his slumber and ripped off what you'd have to call a doozy (aka scientifically, as *flatus*. Or, if you don't believe in science, then fart or ripper may be your preference) amplified by the bare metal chair he was sitting on. We all woke up and the emitter shortly departed.

THE MYSTERIOUS EXPLODING COKE BOTTLE

In November 2008, the community of Chitejé de la Cruz, a few minutes from Chitejé de Garabato, held a small fiesta to celebrate something our agency, SEMARNAT, had accomplished for them. Sonya and I were never sure what that something was, but it involved a semi-formal signing ceremony and lots of food, tequila, pulque, and Coca Cola. As we were saying our goodbyes, a three-liter bottle of Coke on the table alongside Sonya, bloated from the heat, toppled over and ruptured.

The explosion was loud and created momentary chaos and even mild panic. There were murmurings that Los Zetas, considered to be one of the worst of the Mexican drug gangs, had been seen in the area (This is not really true but I do think that Mexicans are always subconsciously wondering if the cartels could move into their area, which they had done, sadly, all over the country). Several people were soda-drenched, including Sonya and an old, arthritic cowboy in a white plastic cowboy hat who couldn't gallop out of the way fast enough.

Coke Explosion in Chitejé de la Cruz

Because she was at the table when it happened, I yelled out in my best, but still lousy, Spanish, "How horrible, how tragic; Sonya must be guilty." The room went silent for a long moment, and then erupted in laughter... not from my attempt at humor (which they mostly didn't understand) but from the relief that Sonya was to blame and not them.

DUNCAN AND BETTY

Many of the forests of México are vanishing, a good portion of them for use as firewood, used for cooking and heating. To help slow the deforestation the Peace Corps is encouraging the use of solar cookers, a project which was instigated by Sonya and became her baby and her most significant project.

To replace wood cooking in low latitude, temperate and tropical countries like México with solar cooking seemed obvious to me, but many women (*the* cooks and bottle washers, of course) we worked with were initially uncertain about the technology. Some even worried about a connection between cancer and solar-cooked food. After several weeks of use, however, they became chattering, enthusiastic supporters. This scenario was the same in every one of the sixteen villages where we introduced the technology.

Solar Cooking Workshop

The solar cooker workshops we conducted were the pinnacle of our Peace Corps experience in the pueblos, in large part because of the consistently wonderful women in the villages we knew, all of whom worked constantly, walked everywhere carrying more weight than I could, and were so grateful, humble and to all appearances, happy. I was always dead tired after each workshop even though Sonya did most of the work. My role was go-fer and comic relief, but I did have one *very* critical function. On the second day of the workshop I baked a chocolate cake in the solar cooker – always a cake from a box.

Old Man with Solar Cooker in Chitejé de la Cruz

The normal village diet is simple but healthy: mostly corn tortillas, beans, rice and fresh vegetables that the villagers grow themselves. Most adult villagers are thin and sinewy because they walk everywhere. But their dietary Achilles heel is sugar – predominantly from Coca Cola and candy. Chocolate cake suits their sugar addiction and mine beautifully.

As I began my "act," I would tell the women that I was using a "receta antigua y secreta de mi familia," an ancient secret family recipe, handed down for many generations from Great-Great Uncle Duncan (Hines) or Great-Great Aunt Betty (Crocker). Most of them had never heard of *Duncan Hines* or *Betty Crocker* because they had never seen a cake mix and possibly had never been inside a supermarket. In their lives, the supermarkets were mule-days away. They usually laughed, I think because they thought I was at least a little nuts, maybe insane depending on the day.

My audience was often mesmerized because the cake only had four ingredients: dry mix, water, eggs and oil. The lack of added sugar perplexed, maybe even annoyed, them, but they would say nothing. Little did they know that more than ample sugar was embedded already in the dry mix. I felt like I was performing a biblical miracle with a cake instead of fish and bread.

As I was cleaning up one afternoon, a woman asked me if she could keep the cake box. "Sure," I said, "but it is going to cost you $1000 pesos ($100 US)." She looked like she was going to cry, so I quickly responded, "But, I will sell it to you for a piece of your first cake." She still didn't understand my blathering Spanish and looked even more tragic, so I just handed her the box.

At one extremely poor, very hot, dusty and windy (aka, almost intolerable) community presentation, after my *coup de grace* – the icing – when people were lining up for their bite, a Mexican-American woman helping us, who spoke fluent Spanish and English, asked me, "David, aren't you going to read the ingredients list off the box to the women before serving up the cake?" "No," I said, "that wasn't part of my plan; they wouldn't understand the long list of chemicals anyway." She retorted, "I feel strongly they need to know how unhealthy a cake mix is, the poisons and all, and that their cakes from scratch are so much healthier." I told her that I didn't think that was necessary or particularly wise, but to be my guest if she felt it was so important.

She proceeded to horrify the women by naming off compounds such as aluminum and chromium, and I think she threw in arsenic to strengthen her case. She talked too fast for me. I am certain she also added something about birth defects. The women were so shocked, likely fearing imminent death or deformed babies that they retreated against the farthest wall, letting their children line up first.

Afterward, Olivia, a Mexican Peace Corps employee, observing our workshop for the first time, said once she heard the ingredients list she felt like wrapping her coat around the cake, running outside and throwing her body over it as it exploded.

TIENE HUEVOS?

Typically, at the close of the first day of the solar cooker workshops, the women split into teams of two or three. On the second day those teams would bring the ingredients to solar cook a dish to be shared with the group for comida that afternoon.

One community, *Barranca del Sordo*, much poorer than the others, had little more than a few chickens and small fields of corn and beans. On the second day, the teams of women coincidently all brought the same thing: eggs. No corn, no beans, no chicken. Just eggs.

In hopes of saving them possible embarrassment as they did a quick comparison of each other's offering, Sonya told the women, "me encantan huevos!" meaning, she thought, "I love eggs." And said with such enthusiasm! The women looked at one another, turned red and bowed their heads to hide their discomfort and their giggles. The word *huevos* in México does translate as eggs, but it also means testicles. So when one is at the market the much safer question to ask is the less personal "Hay huevos?" Are there eggs? Definitely preferred to "Tiene huevos?" Do you have testicles?

BITE ME

I often saw villagers wearing sweatshirts and baseball caps with sometimes inappropriate or offensive English logos. Many were either gifts, brought back from the States by friends and family, or donations from visitors like us. Often, the wearer didn't understand the meaning, and if they did, they didn't care.

Bite Me Hat, Sierra Gorda

In the small community of *El Rucio*, nestled high up in the Sierra Gorda, I saw a hat which read "Bite Me." The woman wearing the hat actually looked like she might bite, but she proved to be very shy. As I've said before, shyness is not uncommon, but once I coerced her to talk, I found she didn't possess a bite, but had a great laugh – a common and very refreshing characteristic of Mexicans. I did not mention her ball cap.

———————

These vignettes describing a few of our experiences hopefully reflect at least one commonality: it was the people themselves who were the essence of those tiny villages, with some pueblos only having a few dozen residents.

Sonya and I found the people of the pueblos, especially the women, to be strong and very dedicated workers but, as a general rule, not aggressive. We encountered a few who had strong, leadership personas, but weren't pushy about it – at least not in our presence. Regardless, they all – men, women, and children – were a cornucopia of kindness and humbleness. And it wasn't just Sonya and me; we heard this story from many other Peace Corps volunteers. And, we never, ever tired of being under their enrapturing spell.

Dance of the Autobuses

By the time we arrived in Querétaro, México, in 2007 as Peace Corps volunteers, my wife and I had already made numerous vacation trips to México, but none to the central plateau region. For perspective, México City is only three hours by intercity bus to the south of Querétaro. As Peace Corps volunteers, we weren't able to drive a car unless we rented it or our sponsor (e.g., a government agency) had the insurance to cover us, which they rarely did.

Consequently, we had come to rely on walking and riding the city and intercity buses, both of which are in abundance in México. The México intercity bus system is likely one of the best in the world, with elegant Volvo and Mercedes buses and superb, punctual service and drivers. Those buses almost always depart and arrive on schedule. From Querétaro, we could catch a bus to México City, on one of several lines, virtually every 20-30 minutes, around the clock. The buses are far more comfortable than airplanes, have bathrooms, and a few serve snacks.

Querétaro City Bus Stop

But the city buses, or autobuses, are another matter altogether. Querétaro has many different companies and routes and hundreds of buses, most which look like old school buses with truncated snouts. The autobuses usually come every 6-8 minutes and cost about 40 cents. This story is about the skilled, but frequently insane, drivers of those buses and their unique styles. As far as I know, the drivers are all men. There may be a female driver cruising somewhere out there in Querétaro, but she is very much alone.

Even though we had used various bus systems on vacations in México in the past, we had never used city buses day after day, month after month, for over three years. Consequently, during our Peace Corps service, we had ample opportunity to observe these cowboys of the inner city and the metal steeds they drove.

In our typical work day, we walked to the bus stop just a few minutes from our house. Normally, the bus got us to work within 20 minutes, depending on the driver and to an extent, the traffic conditions. For many drivers, heavy traffic was not an impediment, but a challenge. A bus ride in a Mexican city like Querétaro, definitely can be a visceral experience, sometimes so visceral it can feel like your stomach is sitting in your throat.

In the States, when you get on a city bus, you stare out the window, snooze, read a book, meditate, or rarely converse with a fellow passenger. Usually the trip is a safe, calming experience, and even soporific – often it can be a time for reflection. This peace of mind is impossible on a city Mexican bus. The non-native passenger may find peace of mind only at a stop light, or when exiting a bus or through dedicated prayer and a continuous massage of one's rosary. I guarantee that you will not die of boredom. You are continuously conscious of participating in a moving theatre. But the driver almost always transports you safely from A to B, seemingly as though his bus were made of very flexible rubber instead of rigid steel, frequently moving at, what feel to be, aircraft speeds. Maneuvering and weaving his bus through the congested streets as if he is riding a motorcycle, he wheels his bus magically within millimeters of other buses, trucks, cars, bicycles and pedestrians. He is *El Rey* – the king of his bus and the streets down which he hurtles; El Rey is the song title of perhaps the most famous machismo song (king of his domain whatever that may be: bus, car, home, family, etc.) ever sung in México by the ranchera king himself, José Alfredo Jiménez (1926-1973).

The autobus experience for the passenger has everything to do with the driver's style, which I have attempted to categorize and describe below. Sometimes, the driver can exhibit several styles on any given journey or even simultaneously. The categories which follow may not be totally rational because they were often observed during times of personal terror, a mental state which I'm sure Mexican riders cannot relate.

1) Speedy Gonzales. Speedy has a penchant for speed at all costs. He is fearless, and it matters not that his non-native passengers may disagree. Speedy maneuvers through traffic with the grace and ease of a Formula One driver. The difference is he controls a bus, not a highly maneuverable race car. Red lights are no obstacle for Speedy, nor are other buses, or "deer in the headlights" pedestrians. Speedy is on a mission from A to Z, and B through Y are only challenges, but he races against no one, at least no one I could ever see.

2) Top Gun. Top Gun watched too many Arnold Schwarzenegger, Charles Bronson or Tom Cruise movies. Like Speedy, part of his mission is speed, but the difference is that he is not so much interested in speed as he is in taking flight, i.e., leaving *terra firma*. If his bus had wings, he would try to fly. He believes he is moving down the runway or the deck of an aircraft carrier and cannot be stopped by anything or anyone even if they are madly waving and screaming directly in his launch trajectory. He just swerves around them or, at the final second, they leap, terrified, out of the way. The frantic pregnant woman with one hand out as though she were trying to stop Top Gun and one hand on her swollen abdomen may get a toot if they're lucky. Gringos with backpacks, faces blood-drained, might get a toot. Cyclists either hug the curb or take a ride to the Pearly Gates. Orange pylons are minor hindrances to be regarded as if he were taking a driving agility exam. Or he simply blows them out of the way. Usually, Top Gun doesn't avoid Grand Canyon-sized potholes, but sees them as tests for his tires and suspension system. If you are one of his passengers, you simply hang on and pray that he will touch down somewhere near your destination.

3) Don Juan. I didn't see too many of these guys (thank God), but to them driving is not their primary mission. Hooking up with one of the beautiful Mexican maidens in a front seat is. Don's eyes only appear to meet the road long enough to keep him on it and avoid collisions. Females, if they are paying attention and riding near the front, should move to the back or get off at the next stop if they want to avoid his gaze or his hand or both. I never saw any women move; they just ignored him.

I was on a bus once with a driver who looked to be about fourteen and could barely see over the wheel. He was the combination of a testosterone-saturated Speedy Gonzales and Don Juan. His *novia* (girlfriend), dressed like a mini-hooker and probably all of twelve, was seated on a large oil can and glued to Juan's right side with her tongue deeply embedded and twirling in his right ear. Every so often they would actually kiss and grope, frequently as Juan had the accelerator buried to the floor. I was definitely jealous – and scared, simultaneously.

4) Gear Grinder. The gear grinder is either deaf or drugged or both. The shifting sound physically hurts deep beyond the eardrum, and the process may take thirty seconds to complete, if it can be completed at all. His gearbox has to have been lacking grease for months, maybe years, with gears looking like Brillo pads. Typically, to complete the shift requires taking both hands off the wheel and staring at the gear shift with malice. If the Gear Grinder isn't on the flat or going downhill, he is in trouble and so are his passengers' eardrums.

5) Lurcher–Braker. These guys haven't been told that the Spanish term *suave*, meaning smooth, can apply to more than just lovemaking. The Lurcher–Braker believes his driving skill is measured by how frequently and rapidly he can move his right foot between the accelerator and the brake. He is determined to get at least one passenger to hurl breakfast or *get* hurled through the front windshield. When you get off his bus, you feel like Frankenstein doing the herky-jerky for a few blocks until you regain your equilibrium.

6) Lane Changer–Light Charger. These characters can't tolerate *status quo*. They loathe their current lane or having another bus in front of them. They accelerate past other buses that try to exit bus stops ahead of them, and if their buses are inches apart and their mirrors are scraping, the Lane Changer guns it, whips ahead, drops in front of his adversary and slams on the brakes. Rarely do they concede position because it is not in the best interest of their machismo. Being forced to whip to an inside lane to avoid being bested may mean they have to bypass their next stop, which also qualifies them for the next category, Rolling Stoppers–No Stoppers. This is not a problem for them even if you are standing at that stop and screaming at the top of your lungs to get attention. They just shrug their shoulders or flip you off. And since they are usually pedal-to-the-metal as they are whipping their mighty steel steed into an engine-screaming froth, they may have to ignore a red light in the process. But, face has been saved.

7) Rolling Stopper–No Stopper. The Rollers open the door for you, but never really come to a full stop. They have watched too many Clint Eastwood leaps onto speeding trains. They may have just changed lanes and gunned past a competitor and aren't about to screech over to get you. They ignore your outstretched arm and screams. They shrug, glare or yell something inarticulate, but they are on a mission. In effect they are saying: get the next #28.

The buses themselves are often pieces of creative genius. Apparently the driver can own the bus, or so I have been told, or the company lets him decorate it just about any way he chooses. Usually, there are various Catholic paraphernalia hanging from the windshield and mirrors, and it is not uncommon to see a pair of baby booties dangling from one of the overhead railings. Huge decals of Calvin and Hobbes, in goggles, or the Road Runner cover the windows with captions confirming that speed is the essence of life.

Once, I was on the bus of a young, super hair-gelled, aspiring artist and lover, who had an air-brushed, larger-than-life sized and very voluptuous semi-nude, painted on the plastic partition behind his seat, facing his passengers. The people in the seat directly behind the driver were at eye level with and about one foot away from her shiny pink thong. On this trip, two nuns sat in that seat.

At times, passengers left behind mementos on the seats or floor – such as wads of Chiclets, urine, or vomit. I´ve attempted to leap for the rear exit door only to find myself *gummed* to my seat.

These scenarios may sound bleak or even terrifying, but in reality, they were not. We came to view these drivers as highway artists. It was as if they were painting a very large Diego Rivera road mural together or conducting a symphony or a ballet involving the hundreds of other buses simultaneously on the same road—literally a dance in which everyone intuitively seemed to know his part. They jockeyed in and out of bus stops within millimeters of each other, entering and exiting at every angle and speed imaginable, only petrifying their gringo passengers while it seemed to me as though most Mexicans riders were not in the least bit concerned. If not sleeping they appeared bored, or chatting or laughing with a neighbor. Without question, I know with unverifiable certainty, they weren't discussing their probability of dying that day in a flaming autobus.

I was glad we didn't have a car. I loved the buses. Despite the fact that México still has too many people and too many cars, particularly in México City, the country's bus system is proof that mass transit can work and work well and can certainly be entertaining, at least for us extraterrestrials.

Guitarist Entertaining Passengers on a City Bus

AMY AND THE CHUPACABRA

February 2009: 10 p.m. Thursday, TAQ (Terminal Autobuses Querétaro).

As we leave the Querétaro bus station, through the frosty bus window, I can see the cold February star-studded night sky. We are heading west for San Blas in the Pacific coastal state of Nayarit. Sonya and I have become accustomed to these all-night bus rides and as long as we adequately drug ourselves for sleep, we have found that the night rides are usually pretty enjoyable. It depends on several factors including the bus line, the driver, the route, and occasionally the passengers. With the starry night sky and Dramamine, this trip portends to be idyllic, maybe even hallucinogenic. The bus ride to Tepic—the preliminary stretch—is about eight hours.

3 a.m. Friday, in the mountains somewhere in the clouds, still east of Tepic.

The driver has been playing very loud ranchera music since about 1:30 a.m., despite my earlier timid request to reduce the volume. We might as well have been in the front row at a live José Alfredo Jiménez performance. When I make my case to him that I can't sleep, he stares at me as if I'm visiting his bus from the *Starship Enterprise*. He says and does nothing. Later, he benevolently shuts the music off when we arrived at the terminal in Tepic at 6 a.m. Add that to the fact that he has the AC redlined, making the bus effectively a Birds Eye frozen peas rig as we pass through the mountains. I think to myself, sure, why not see if you can get ice on *both* sides of the windows? The Mexicans don't notice because they are comatose, swaddled in layers of sweatshirts and coats. Even on the hottest of México days they wear at least a hoodie and wool stocking cap —more often than not black in color. You seldom see shorts on Mexicans. I'm so damned cold that I think I'm going into hypothermia and will have to be carried off the bus like a big chilled lizard, unable to move under my own power. Since we are going to the San Blas beach, I didn't think to bring any of my Antarctic gear, so I envision myself on that beach, basking to elevate my body temperature so I can crawl, and walk crab-like to the water's edge. Sonya is zonked out beside me; she may actually be in hibernation. Her snoring competes with the blasting ranchera music, creating a sleep-retardant cacophony of dissonant sounds.

6 a.m. Friday, bus terminal, Tepic.

We have just arrived in Tepic, the capital of the state of Nayarit, and we are both in such a Dramamined state that all we can do is sit, shivering in the cracked plastic chairs as we wait for that yellow ball of fire to blast through the window and thaw our bones. Of course there is no central heating in the terminal; there never is in México. People learn to operate keyboards wearing mittens and swaddled in heavy coats. They look like mummies frozen in front of their computers.

Besides the sun, we are also waiting for the San Blas ticket office to open. We try to keep from nodding off, but can only talk through clenched teeth because our jaw muscles haven't thawed yet. I don't even have the clarity of mind or energy to buy a bus terminal donut, a Mexican paragon of gastronomic pastry delight. Why bus station donuts? The quintessential donut deep fry standards may exist in México, but are universally ignored, so donuts can be so dry as to choke you or so greasy they drip. Except, for some inexplicable reason, one can get a real donut at bus terminals. We console ourselves with the fact that the San Blas beaches and perpetual sun lay downhill and only an hour west.

8 a.m. Thursday, San Blas.

We got here around 7:00, and already have eaten at McDonalds. Not the golden arches variety – which they do have all over México but not in San Blas. This McDonalds is a local norteamericano hangout reputed to have the best food in town – which we find highly questionable. We order *frijoles* and *huevos*. Now, after dragging our luggage all over San Blas, which is small, we have found Amy's street and her pad. Amy is a good friend and another PC volunteer who is studying aspects of mangrove marshes along the state of Nayarit's coastline.

Her passion is scuba diving, and she claims that if she is away from open water more than a day, she will put on her wetsuit, tanks, and mask and get in the shower. She has *Nemo* stickers plastered on her shower wall. If asked to sum up Amy's character in one sentence: she has a porcupine exterior with a marshmallow interior.

7 p.m. Friday.

We are drinking rum and Cokes while Sonya is brushing Amy's adopted daschund, Scooby. Scooby appears to seriously love it. Scooby, short for Scooby Doo – and Amy likes to call him Scoob - which is what I'll call him, is not your typical Mexican street mongrel; he is very classy, and gives every appearance of being convinced, despite his diminutive size, that he is the most sought-after male dog in town when darkness descends on San Blas. Cuddled in his toasty little doggy sofa at Amy's during the day, he conserves his energy for his nightly forays on the streets of San Blas. His nighttime cruising appears to have two purposes: a) to reaffirm that *all* of San Blas is his domain and b) to hopefully "hook up" with unsuspecting poochitas of all sizes and shapes. From Scoob's ground-hugging, lowrider perspective, the poochitas all tower over him. But, according to Amy, that is no deterrent—to either aspiring nocturnal partner. Apparently, several wannabe Scoobs roam San Blas, but there is only one Scoob.

Scoob

Amy has unofficially adopted Scoob because his real owner abuses him. Because Scoob spends much of his idle time with Amy, his owner is demanding what might be described as a rental fee, to be augmented if he sires any offspring. This evening, we watch Scoob's technique as we stroll behind him through the streets of San Blas. He struts his way around potholes that must seem like Grand Canyons to him, and he challenges *all* males, without regard to size, who even look like they are going to question his status as the canine king of San Blas.

Amy's apartment is small and unique. It isn't uncommon for Peace Corps volunteers to have tiny places, but her place has some features that truly place it in a class of its own and are worthy of elaboration. She had warned us that we would all be sleeping in the same tiny bedroom, and that she would give us her bed because she loved her hammock, which hung about a foot away from my side of the bed. Fortunately, she didn't go to bed until 3 a.m., about six hours past our bedtime, so her snoring never really disturbed me, but when she flipped in my direction, her rum and Coke breath did.

The kitchen is tiny and doesn't present any issues unless you are cooking for more than one. But tonight, when I offer to do the dishes, I discover the kitchen's real Achilles heel: the sink. On quick glance it looks fine; a deep, newly installed, porcelain double sink. Great, I think.

But when Amy swears and kicks it, I look a little closer. No drain. That's right, no drain. The landlord, neighbor, fisherman and friend, Ruben, remodeled the kitchen and the bathroom on Amy's request, but he took some shortcuts to save cost and labor time. As a consequence, one has to use a big sponge and a bucket after doing the dishes. The dishwater goes onto the street.

Amy and a Friend

6:00 a.m. Saturday.

The bathroom is an even more dramatic plumbing statement than the kitchen sink. Amy refers to it as a "Ruben" Goldberg. While it is still dark outside, I have enjoyed my first cup of coffee and now have crammed myself into her tiny bathroom. The plumbing of the toilet has been described by Amy as being flush-challenged; the pipe diameter is small—too small for normal defecation unless you are a shrew. Solids require a bucket brigade from an already over-stressed kitchen, a stirrer and lots of time, which we do not have in abundance this morning because Ruben is waiting to take us out in his fishing boat. According to Amy, what happened was that Ruben installed a one inch pipe instead of the normal three inches. Whatever it was, it didn't even meet the San Blas city codes, which I'm sure, if they exist, are very loose.

8 a.m. Saturday, Ruben's panga.

The last time I had been on the ocean fishing was as a kid somewhere off the Maine coast, but the boat was a lot bigger than Ruben's and more seaworthy. I got seasick then so I'm a little worried as we head out. Ruben had told us to be ready to leave for the docks by 7:00. After a five minute breakfast, five minute shower, and fifty minute flushing, we left in the back of Ruben's pickup, heading into the gray dawn. As we were departing, Scoob appeared out of nowhere from the shrubbery with a three-legged female partner, and they both chased us down to the wharf, hopping along in the dust of the pickup. They somehow managed to stay up with us.

When we reach Ruben's fishing boat, or *panga*, we are a little concerned because the weather is foggy, but Ruben assures us that it would burn off. We motor down the channel alongside the rather famous San Blas fleet, Scoob and companion hopping down the road beside us. Amy worries that Scoob will jump into the water and drown, so we turn around to rescue him. But just as we do, he quits and heads home.

As we head into open water—dead calm—the morning fog settles down like a veil over the sea surface so we can't see past the bow, where Amy is sound asleep. Sonya's and my primary goal was to see whales and anything else resembling the natural world; we are starved to see some wildlife, but particularly marine life, which makes perfect sense being as how we are in the middle of the ocean. Ruben, on the other hand, wants to catch fish. Big fish. The sea is placid until we get out past the islands and then we hit a little chop. We head west for almost an hour with the only signs of life the frigate birds gliding overhead. No whales. No sailfish. No marlin. No sea turtles.

No manta rays.

Then a few more miles out we hit the "garbage stream," literally a stream of food and plastic that spews out of an estuary a few miles north of San Blas. At that point Ruben throttles down and we start weaving in and out of the garbage and then we begin seeing everything pretty much simultaneously. As if on cue from Walt Disney, the fog lifts, the sun burns through, and the humpback whale pods start sliding to the surface and blowing. Everywhere. It is a true ecological pyramid. The smaller fish are feeding on the garbage and invertebrates, the bigger fish are feeding on the smaller fish and the turtles are floating in the flotsam and feeding on whatever, while gulls fish from perches on the turtles' shells.

Humpback Whale

Seagull Perched on Sea Turtle

It becomes a magical wonderland of marine life. The marlin and sailfish are coming close enough to the panga to touch, and they are big and Ruben is salivating. They do not want his bait even though Ruben literally bangs them on their snouts with it. They cruise just below the surface, knifing a wake with their dorsal fin like they think they are great white sharks. *Que dia fabulosa!* We see everything we came to see but a giant squid. We catch one small fish. Ruben is really embarrassed, but Sonya and I think we have died and gone to biologists' heaven.

3 p.m. Saturday.

As we pull into Ruben's slip we are hot, tired, hungry and thirsty, but guess who is waiting patiently for us in the hot sun? Scoob. Three Leg is nowhere to be seen; probably snoozing from a night of revelry with the Scoob. Instead, lying alongside Scoob is a big female German shepherd, and they both look very relaxed as they puff on Lucky Strikes. We go back to Amy's, and Ruben is feeling very low about all the big ones that got away, so he goes directly to his frozen marlin stash and pulls out a few steaks that I grill on his extremely unstable sidewalk grill. Ruben's mom watches warily, advising my every move.

Ruben's Mom

11:30 a.m. Monday, Tepic bus terminal.
Following our day on the high seas, we are
waiting at the bus station for the bus to La
Bajada, a town in the nearby coastal mountains to
go hiking. *Everyone* told us to wait at an obscure
bus stop across town, but they failed to mention
that the buses *only* run every hour and *only* from
the terminal on Sundays. We found, early on, that
Mexicans like to give foreigners directions, even
if they are wrong. They hate to say "No."

On our trek, we managed to see some colorful
woodland birds and visit the cocodrilero
(crocodile refuge) where we stared transfixed at
some really big teeth a few inches away through a
flimsy chicken-wire fence. There is a sign there
that says if you wrestle one and aren't eaten, you
get your entrance fee returned. Despite my frugal
nature, I wasn't tempted.

Now, in Tepic, we wait for the bus to
Guadalajara. We're tired and somewhat dejected
having said goodbye to Amy and the Scoob. Amy
is certainly one of our favorite people. In
Guadalajara, several hours hence, we will transfer
buses to Querétaro—another several hours past
Guadalajara.

Perhaps you are wondering why I haven't
mentioned the whatever-it-is chupacabra in the
title. Well, I love the word, the legend and the

weird psychedelic carvings. A chupacabra is a mythical beast of the Americas (even Texas, which makes sense) that is reputed to suck the blood of livestock, particularly goats. The alebrije carvers of Oaxaca, México, have produced some wonderfully nightmarish variations.

Chupacabra

I thought it made a compelling, if totally irrelevant, title. I wanted to put chupacabras in some story because they captured my fancy. Let me make it clear that our weekend with Amy was anything but a nightmare; quite to the contrary. Admittedly, I am anxious to get back to our casita in Querétaro where we have a normal bathroom and kitchen. Other than that detail, it was truly one of those times when magic descended upon us in México and left us with memories never to be forgotten.

Papa Ricardo
(NOVEMBER 16, 1942 – APRIL 27, 2010)
"SI, MI VIDA, LO QUE TU DIGAS"

After a few tequilas, with a straight face, he asked me who I thought had the last word in a Mexican matrimonial argument: the husband or the wife. Knowing that most Mexican families are strongly matriarchal, I answered that most likely it was the wife. "No," said Ricardo, "the Mexican husband *ALWAYS* has the final word." "And what is that?" I asked. "Si, mi vida, lo que tu digas," he said with a rumbling chuckle. "Yes, my love, whatever you say."

In what remains of this short portrait, I want to continue to share some aspects of Ricardo Lepe's personality, which was dominated by humor. Having said that, I find it extremely difficult to sketch a funny human being with words and photos; humor has everything to do with nuances which can only be captured live or on video. Regardless the short comings of this portrayal, Ricardo left a huge impression on me. Ricardo celebrated his 67th birthday on November 16, 2009, in true Mexican fashion: a small fiesta with family, friends, a trio of guitar players and a very local famous singer – his lifetime companion, Maria Zepeda. Maria's singing began as passable, but improved with each *caballito* of tequila, the traditional super shot. A caballito of tequila is frequently drunk the macho way by both men and women – neat and quick.

Even though Ricardo was only three months my senior, he was "Papá" to me. This stemmed largely from the fact that as part of the first three months of Peace Corps training, the Lepe Zepedas became our Mexican family. We lived with them, and Maria and Ricardo became our Mexican mamá and papá, their adult children, our siblings.

Ricardo

94

Ricardo was a great teacher of Mexican culture over the 2 1/2 years we knew him. He especially taught us about Mexican humor, all by example. He was a virtuoso in a culture that placed a very high premium on comic relief. Mexicans seem addicted to fun, and humor is a huge component of that. Everyone knew, remembered and told jokes of all types. The most painful to listen to for non-Spanish speakers were the shaggy dog stories that went on FOREVER, and were rarely, if ever, funny – at least to us English speakers. When the punch line was mercifully delivered, you would be the only person standing, mouth agape, usually because you didn't know that it was the punch line while everyone else would be doubled over in convulsions of laughter.

Ricardo's humor may, in part, have been due to his hangdog, Rodney Dangerfield deadpan expression. He was modestly overweight and even looked somewhat like Dangerfield. This tended to give me a warm, confident feeling when I was around him. It made me wish at times he'd pull me in and smother me in his bear-like embrace.

Prior to our arrival in México, the Peace Corps had arranged for all volunteers to live with a host family for three months. We were all nervous about where and with whom we would be living. We met our hosts, Papá Ricardo and Mamá Maria with some anxiety, on our second day in México, in the lobby of the Peace Corps office. Host families were there to meet their volunteers and escort them to their new homes. Ricardo grabbed our bags and began lugging them to his little car. Somewhere in that process, they both gave us huge welcoming hugs. Maria almost immediately told Sonya in the back seat during the short drive to their and our new home, "We love you." Sonya was a little taken aback, but she instinctually knew that Maria meant it. Their home was on Alcatraz Street. Alcatraz, of course, is a famous prison in the United States, but in Spanish, paradoxically, it is a flower, a calla lily.

Ricardo with the Author

Sonya at a Restaurant with Ricardo and Maria

That first evening, we sat in their living room, and Ricardo and Maria introduced us to themselves as well as to *ponche*. Ponche is a traditional, homemade Mexican Christmas punch made with brandy and various fruits, including apples, oranges, guavas, and *tejocotes* (apple-pear combo), and brown sugar or *pilloncillo*, and cinnamon. But Ricardo also made his own special pomegranate and tequila concoction, which we liberally sampled. It was then that we became acutely aware of Ricardo's excellent sense of humor.

After a few glasses of ponche and Ricardo's home brew, we were feeling like we'd known each other for years despite the language barrier. We wandered downtown for an introduction to Querétaro's night

97

life. Even though it has been a decade since that first day with the Lepe Zepeda family, my recollection of it is crystal clear and not lacking considerable emotion.

With our three months of training completed, we needed to move out of the Lepe Zepeda's home into more permanent quarters. It would have been a very sad day indeed had it not been for the fact that we moved just around the corner to Magnolias Street, only five minutes walk away. We got to see our adopted family regularly. Ricardo continued to be my favorite and most colorful Mexican friend.

Jokes, particularly *doble sentidos* (two interpretations), are a Mexican obsession. You cannot really appreciate the Mexican office environment or a fiesta without being able to tell and enjoy jokes, especially doble sentidos. When I attempted to retell a Mexican joke or the rare one of our own that I remembered or at least remembered everything except the most important part, the punchline, Mexicans were always polite and pretended to enjoy it, usually with a soft chuckle. Most of the time they were clueless as to the meaning, which was more likely due to my weak joke-telling and language skills. Sonya was better at both, so I functioned best as her laugh track, especially if her joke looked like it was going to flop.

Of all the jokes Ricardo told me, two stand out in my mind, and I actually remember their most critical details. Most likely due to Ricardo's skill, these two jokes never failed to make us laugh each time we begged him to retell them. Both are about abused –

or allegedly abused – husbands, a common theme in Mexican jokes. One is the story of a baseball catcher, Carlos, who habitually returned home drunk after games and continually got smacked across the head by his wife, Margarita, who kept a bat by the door for just such occasions. Carlos never got through the door if he was drunk – regardless whether the team had won or lost. Finally after one night when he had taken an exceptionally bad beating, one of his teammates recommended, "Carlos, why don't you go back to the locker room and get your catcher's mask and wear it home for protection tonight?" Carlos thought that was a great idea, so he did just that. When his wife came to the door, she looked at him weaving around on the stoop with his mask on and screamed, "Foul ball!" Up flew Carlos's mask and "smack" went Margarita's bat.

The second joke is about José, a jobless guy whose wife, Lupita, wants a divorce because José doesn't do anything around the house except sit, watch TV and drink beer, with the family cat and dog snoozing on either side of his feet. He realizes he needs to see his priest to avert the divorce. After hearing his story, the priest says, "Well, José, why don't you do some jobs around the house if you really want to save your marriage? You don't work and your wife does." José responds, "I can't. I can't even get up from my Lazy Boy recliner." "What do you mean?" says the priest, "you're not an invalid." José counters, "Well, let me explain. In my left hand

I have the remote, in my right hand the beer bottle, with my left foot I'm scratching the cat, and with my right foot the dog." Apparently, neither man in either story tried, "Si, mi vida, lo que tu digas."

Ricardo had a fascination for *Sponge Bob*, the bizarre children's cartoon character, watching it with his grandchildren or even alone. I never saw it, but he did talk about Bob frequently. His pronunciation of "Spongay Boob" brings a smile to my face even now. I can still hear him, in his gravelly bass voice, telling me about Bob's latest absurd antics.

Five months following his birthday fiesta, Papá Ricardo was dead of cancer. Maria invited us to visit Ricardo a week before his death, and he was still telling jokes, albeit in a more subdued voice, from his bottomless fountain of humor. I will always miss him, not just for his comedic nature, but for the truly wonderful, loving and generous person he was. He and Maria, and their eldest son, Beto, who lived with his parents at the time, Beto's brothers and sons, accepted Sonya and me as members of their family from that very first moment we left the Peace Corps headquarters and drove home in their car.

At his wake, Sonya and I were surprised not only that it was held the very same day of his death, but to discover that very few people, if any, appeared to be grieving. In fact, most were even laughing and telling Ricardo stories, virtually none of which I understood. Consistent with the *Dia de los Muertos* (Day of the Dead) celebration and Mexican philosophy, the wake revealed the striking difference between the way we Americans and the Mexicans view death. To Mexicans – predominantly Catholic – death is intended to be a celebration of life on earth, but perhaps more importantly, a better life ahead in heaven. That isn't to say there wasn't sadness and grieving; there definitely was at the somber mass held later for Ricardo, but even then the music theme was rock.

In consideration of death, of all the holidays and fiestas that Mexicans celebrate, the one that impresses me the most is Dia de los Muertos, held the two days following Halloween, November 1-2. I doubt we will ever celebrate in our country the demise of our loved ones by dancing, eating and drinking on their graves – and telling jokes. It is in no way macabre, but rather a very healthy way to keep deceased loved ones still in the minds and discussions of the living. As far as Ricardo is concerned, I will continue to celebrate his life by telling his story, and, however poorly, frequently trying to tell his jokes – if I don't forget the punch lines.

THREE SQUARES, THREE PESOS

About two years into our stay in México, we'd come to realize that our intestinal fauna still occasionally held us ransom and hadn't completely accepted a vastly different cuisine containing a more provocative diversity of little creatures than our guts were accustomed to. It is difficult to reason with those microscopic feisty little devils when you can't even see them let alone talk or write to them. I once made them a juicy peace offering of *chicharrón*, deep fried pig skin, in hopes of a faster acclimation to the Mexican diet. Chicharrón can be prepared hot and slimy or dry and crispy. In the United States, we call the dry version pork rind. I dislike both, particularly the hot and slimy version, but I reasoned the chicharrón would have lots of new bacteria to introduce to my gut mix. It didn't work.

The entire time we lived in México, we were subject to fairly regular episodes of *La Turista,* a.k.a., Montezuma's Revenge, Green Apple Two Step, Sharts, Squirts, Screaming Mimis, or my personal favorite, the Peace Corps unofficial term among volunteers, *Splatterfoot.* The Peace Corps' recommended antidote, *Pepto-Bismol,* in my experience does absolutely nothing except taste like *Black Jack* gum or ouzo, the powerful Greek anise drink, and turn your tongue and effluent black. Not a pleasant mental image, but one that needs to be said.

One of our Peace Corps colleagues claimed that he had been in a permanent state of Splatterfoot for his entire two years of service in México. We all found it rather odd that our friend remained surprisingly healthy looking and even put on some significant weight over the two years. Another volunteer claimed she was "visited" at exactly two week intervals. According to her it made absolutely no difference what she had been eating. Blam! The predictability was a little hard for me to swallow (pun intended) but the urgency was not.

Throughout our time in México, periodically Sonya and I would be lured into eating Mexican road food especially on long bus rides. Incredibly tasty, it was not unlike our fast foods, but usually much healthier and tastier, which isn't difficult to imagine—but not always from the microorganism perspective. Often we had no option unless we chose to starve. It would happen when we were en route to/from a project or village and our chauffer would suggest stopping at a roadside stand to eat *tacos de carnitas* (shredded pork with seasoning). Temporary gastronomic ecstasy along the roadside often had dire consequences later that night when one of us would be in the fetal position, shaking under the covers from chills or draped over the porcelain queen in our tiny bathroom in agony.

The only positive thing about Splatterfoot was its

short life span. Usually, in twenty-four hours on a regimen of tea, bananas, saltines and sleep, you would be weak but feel okay. At times, its onset could strike blindingly fast, with little warning, and depending upon where you were at the time, that could be problematic. This saga is about one of those memorable moments when it was indeed problematic.

Sonya and I often took the autobus across town to our work at the SEMARNAT state office. Depending on traffic and the maneuvering skills of the bus driver, it generally took about twenty minutes to make the trip. One particularly beautiful spring morning in 2009, we had planned to stop en route at Alameda Park, located along the bus route and one of the most beautiful of all the parks in the city because of its giant old shady eucalyptus trees. Our plan was to help our SEMARNAT colleagues with an annual environmental education fair for school children. SEMARNAT has a major nationwide environmental education responsibility, the initial reason for our work with SEMARNAT.

Environmental education of school children is a big commitment in México, in many ways more so than in the States. That is not to imply that this education makes any difference to the landscape (littering, deforestation, erosion, etc.). That is in part because the vast majority of Mexicans live on a few dollars a day and understandably can't make conservation and environmental responsibility a top priority. Furthermore, in most communities, large and small, the infrastructure, such as regular trash collection or sewage treatment facilities, may likely be nonexistent. The implementation of what children learn in school may be sorely lacking. But we did marvel at the impressive level of environmental awareness, even among uneducated villagers. On more than one occasion, I had very sophisticated discussions about climate change or biodiversity with people I would have never guessed would have had an interest let alone an understanding of the concepts. Much of that may have had to do with their closeness to the land and distance from distracting technology, like television, movies, tractors, phones and TVs. Their hands and bare feet may have literally been in contact with the earth most of the day.

We had been told by our SEMARNAT colleagues that the environmental fair had some relevant material, but perhaps the biggest draw, certainly from the children's perspective, was the caged animals on display. The description we'd heard prior to our arrival at Alameda Park sounded like a true environmental fair with native species on display rather than a miniature version of Barnum & Bailey. I expected to see some rare endemic Mexican species, like the jaguar and military macaws. As it turned out, most of the animals on display not only were not native to México, they weren't even native to the western hemisphere. I saw one emaciated Bengal tiger and a pacing, panting, hairless hyena. They did have one badly mangled nine-banded armadillo, which is native and looked like he had encountered a viscious dog or been hit by a car. Regardless, the kids could have cared less where the beasts came from; they loved them. And, because saving México's incredible biodiversity is an important goal of SEMARNAT, I guess having anything living was better than stuffed specimens. The common practice in México, as well as much of Latin America, has been, historically speaking, to kill everything that runs, crawls, flies or slithers.

Alameda Park was probably a ten minute bus ride from our house. About nine minutes into that ride on that gorgeous spring morning, I started to have serious abdominal cramping. A minute later, when we reached the park stop, without time for an explanation to Sonya, I was off the bus and moving across the busy Zaragoza Avenue, dodging traffic, heading toward the park on the opposite side. All the time, I was thinking that I might have to dive behind one of the big eucalyptus trees if a public restroom was not readily accessible. I had left Sonya, without explanation, standing immobile and confused at the bus stop. Alameda is popular with lovers of all ages, at any time of day, and lots of senior voyeurs sit on the benches gawking at the lovers. Not many hiding places.

I moved into the cover of the trees as swiftly as my condition would allow, and as I did I grabbed a small kid who confirmed there was indeed a public restroom and pointed me toward it. *Gracias a Dios*, the restroom was close. Public restrooms in México are not a given like they are in United States parks. At least not in the parks I visited. If there is one, there is almost always a little old lady or a small child guarding the entrance, charging a few pesos to get into the restroom. In return, she (or he) gives you a few single ply squares of toilet paper whether you need it or not. I completely understand why; it provides jobs. In my experience, I never found a roll or two of TP in public stalls in México. And what the TP lady doles out is usually barely enough for a very conservative, very small child. Coincidently, I had EXACTLY three pesos in my pocket which was the charge for three squares: one peso per square. Single ply.

After plopping down my pesos, and whipping my three squares from her claw, I made it to the nearest stall, which fortunately was empty, and let fly. I needed an entire roll, and I had three squares. I needed more; a lot more. With my pants still loose, I went to the restroom door, and timidly stuck my head around the corner and whimpered my urgent needs to señora TP. I was incredibly embarrassed, and fortunately, there was no one else around but her. With lips pursed, she hunkered even deeper behind her desk with her beady little eyes aimed in my direction and her tiny hands protecting her neat little stacks of three squares. Even with my protestations, it was clear she wasn't going to part with even one more square unless I produced the pesos. In my weak and highly stressed Spanish, I explained that my wife was "just over there" and I could pay triplicate for the paper in a few minutes, but I needed a loaner of several stacks – *muy rapido*! Her response? "Lo siento, señor, pero cuesta tres pesos por papel hygenico." "I'm sorry, sir, but it costs three pesos for the toilet paper." The topic was not open for discussion.

Three Squares of Toilet Paper with Three Pesos

She gave me no choice but to cover the intervening space between us as fast as my GI track would permit and lunge past her to steal several of her neat little piles.

Señora TP was probably 5 feet tall, and if necessary, I was prepared to wrestle her to the ground for the paper. I still remembered some takedown moves from my years as a high school wrestler. Fortunately – and wisely for her – she chose not to chase me back to my stall. The look in my eyes was enough to discourage her.

Toilet Paper Lady at a Public Restroom

My day could only improve, and for the most part, it did. I was able to enjoy the fair in reasonable comfort with only a few more dashes to visit the señora. I had tipped her handsomely because Sonya had given me a pocketful of spare pesos, so the señora seemed to be trying to be cordial; she was making a bundle of pesos off me. Furthermore, she was more preoccupied with arranging her tiny piles than paying attention to me.

Future Restroom Attendant with Mother??

As we left Alameda Park that day, we passed the restroom and I noticed the señora was gone. However, I encountered what might have been her future replacement with his mom, maybe getting early on-the-job training.

CHRISTMAS IN BARRANCA DEL SORDO

In November 2010, approaching the end of our time in México, Sonya and I made our first visit to Barranca del Sordo to give a solar cooker workshop to twenty families. Barranca del Sordo means "canyon of the deaf." Even though I tactfully asked several villagers, I never got an answer as to the origin of the name. My initial reaction was that the entire community was deaf and didn't hear me. The greater likelihood was that they didn't understand my still marginal Spanish because they smiled, which suggested they heard *something*. Sordo, as I shall henceforth call it, was about two hours southeast of Querétaro and located on the opposing slopes of a small, very arid desert canyon, not far from the huge Zimapan Reservoir and the river separating the states of Hidalgo and Querétaro.

After over a year of visiting about fifteen or so small pueblos in central México, we were struck by several unique characteristics of Sordo. First, the surrounding habitat was arid and void of most native trees. We were accustomed to the desert in this part of México, but usually the pueblos had plenty of trees and were situated along perennial streams. In Sordo, a smattering of exotic evergreens grew around a few homes and some native willows survived along the dry stream bed. There was little soil to speak of except that which had eroded off the slopes into the flood plain where they had planted their spindly, dryland corn. I saw no evidence of irrigation. Any native trees or woody shrubs that might have existed in the area had long ago been cut for firewood. The people were still dependent on wood for cooking and heat, so unless they wanted to cut their few shade trees, they had to travel high into the mountains, several hours away by burro, to find it.

Second, the pueblo was painfully poor, more so than we had ever seen before. They told us that if they bought firewood, which I assumed they rarely did, it would cost them about $15 United States per burro load, more than a family's monthly income. Their diet (we soon were to discover), consisted of eggs, an occasional geriatric chicken, tortillas and beans. We didn't see any evidence of vegetable gardens as we had in other rural communities, likely due to the lack of irrigation water.

Third, their physical appearance was different. The people, particularly the women, of all the rural communities we had previously visited were not uncommonly a little overweight, but never as obese as city dwellers. In contrast, the adults of Sordo were skinny and sinewy, most likely from lack of diet diversity, hard physical labor, and a lot of hill walking.

And finally, their shyness and humbleness were palpable – especially among the adults. Initially, the town gave the impression of being deserted. They didn't seem to socialize much. Everyone appeared to work continuously. Regardless, they would magically appear, almost running as if they had a surplus of energy, within minutes of our arrival. Visitors of any kind were an anomaly in Sordo and drew the townsfolk in like sharks to fresh blood, but slightly less intimidating.

The children didn't share their parents' shyness. It wasn't uncommon for them to initially hide behind their mothers' skirts, particularly when our cameras came out, but once any one of them saw his or her own photo, they *all* wanted theirs taken – as many times as you were willing to press the shutter.

Five Girls in Barranca del Sordo

Rural pueblo reticence was very common, but the adults of Sordo took it to another level. We simply could not get them to talk. For example, on the second day of solar cooker workshops, once the women had their cookers, they were asked to return the next day with the ingredients to cook a dish of their own choosing in their new cooker for sharing with their fellow villagers. In Sordo, they said nothing to us about their assignment and probably nothing to each other, but they *all* brought eggs to boil that second day. That was our first clue that their diet was limited. At least we knew they had chickens, which I assume were eventually eaten once they quit laying.

Their timidity made me uncomfortable. On the second day of the workshop, when I did my ever-popular Betty Crocker – Duncan Hines solar cake baking demo, as I told about in *Pueblo Moments*, the women of any other pueblo would normally be giggling and whispering among themselves, whether they totally understood it or not. But the women of Sordo just looked at me; not even the hint of a smile on any of their faces. Again I asked myself: were they really all deaf? My Spanish had survived many other Betty and Duncan tellings with at least smattering of tittering, but this place was uniquely stoic!

When Sonya and I returned to Sordo for the follow-up after about a month of them hopefully using their cookers, it was in early December, dark at 5 p.m., very cold, and very windy. It was the kind of cold that only a desert can possess in winter – piercing to the bone. This time, they knew we were coming and all twenty families – husbands, if they were around – always the children and the dogs, and of course, the women, were waiting patiently, packed in the tiny schoolroom when we arrived. It was a full house.

The Author Demonstrating a Solar Cooker

After Sonya made small talk for a few minutes about our journey from Querétaro, and other pueblos' solar cooking experiences, just to set the audience at ease, which it always had in the past, she then asked for volunteers to tell of their cooking experiences, good or bad. No one raised a hand. That *was* a first. The room went deadly silent; they sat there and just looked at us. She waited. Blank stares looked back at her. I was trying to evaporate in the corner. Taking the silence as lack of interest, Sonya rather severely rebuked them, saying that the cookers were basically free and if anyone wanted to return theirs, their $5 would be refunded. Still dead silence, but no one asked for money back.

It looked like it was going to be a standoff until in desperation we broke up into groups and started to question them individually. Then we discovered how hastily we had misjudged them. Quietly, very quietly, the women and the occasional man beamed as they talked about the soup or the rice dish they had made. So they didn't just eat eggs! All very simple dishes – a few contained chicken, probably tender as rubber, but most of the dishes were meatless.

Some of them were almost on the verge of tears as they talked about how much they loved their cooker and its capabilities. In that final hour, they stole our hearts like no other pueblo had ever done. I about fainted when several of the women asked, barely above a whisper, and totally straight-faced, "¿Por favor, podría darnos la receta antigua de pastel de chocolate de su famoso bisabuelos Betty y Duncan?" "Please, would you give us the ancient chocolate cake recipe of your famous great grandparents, Betty and Duncan?" They obviously had been paying closer attention than I previously thought.

Driving back to Querétaro that evening we got into a discussion with our government friend who chauffeured us from the town of Cadereyta about what Christmas must be like in Sordo. It sounded bleak. So we decided perhaps we could help Sordo that Christmas with SEMARNAT employee donations of food, clothing and toys. We calculated a population of about ninety in Sordo, about fifty of those children.

Christmas in Barraca del Sordo

We put a tree up in the SEMARNAT lobby and sent out an announcement and waited. Unlike the States, donating and volunteering is not common in México.

By Wednesday, December 15, two days before our trip to Sordo and the last work day before the holiday, the sheet under the tree was bare. I went to the supermarket and bought every box they had of Duncan and Betty cake mixes and managed enough for two per family. I thought I might need to buy everything because Sordo was definitely expecting Santa to pay them a visit. However, by Friday morning, gifts mysteriously had appeared and were even spilling into the hallway. Yet another example of a Mexican "miracle," aka, Mexican procrastination – a national trait.

On that day, a gorgeous clear day with the wind kicking up dust devils in the desert, we drove to Sordo, stopping in Cadereyta to buy three clay piñatas and fill them with candy and small toys. The villagers were patiently waiting at the schoolhouse, many of them dressed in their best. The parents and older teenagers stood around the fringe, mesmerized by the frenzied smaller children as they pulverized the three piñatas in rapid succession, racing screaming to the fallen candy as if it would vaporize if they didn't get to it. While the children were stuffing their pockets, I momentarily caught the eye of the community representative, Juana, a young woman perhaps in her late thirties, while she was laughing at the children's exuberance and ever so quickly smiling at me, before averting her eyes to the ground.

Sign at Highway Turnoff to Barranca del Sordo

Before our service ended and we left México that next spring, we made one final trip to Sordo to see how they were doing with their cookers. Again, they knew we were coming and a handful of women met us at Juana's house. Juana had a big plastic pitcher of guava juice, popularly called *agua fresca*, sitting out for us beside a stack of plastic glasses. For a few minutes we talked quietly with them about their cooker experiences. As we started to take our leave, Juana gently tugged on Sonya's sleeve, and as Sonya turned back toward her, Juana handed her a carefully rolled bundle of multi-colored cloth. "Hice este mantel para Ud. y Don David," she whispered, looking toward the floor. "I made this tablecloth for you and Don David." It likely represented several long days of work. Sonya and I said very little to each other on the drive back to Querétaro. As we reached the paved highway and the sign directing one to Sordo, I vividly recall staring out the car window as if in a trance and thinking that the desert didn't look quite as hostile as it did on previous visits.

LA CASITA

I am writing this a week after departing México, several days following our official Peace Corps México program closure day, April 7, 2011. Before leaving we were given several *despedidas*, or farewell parties. I do not like goodbyes anymore than most people, but there are those infrequent exceptions and one occurred while we were living in México. I didn't mind bidding farewell to one guest who overstayed his México visit to *La Casita*, the little house, *our* little house, which had only one tiny bathroom. Despite repeatedly telling him that in México you *only* leave bodily products in the toilet and paper goes in the wastebasket, he continued to throw TP into the toilet and clogging the system. He was a little slow to get the message until I finally said, in exasperation, "Weren't you planning to leave TODAY? If not, keep in mind you have one more flush!"

When we terminated our service with Peace Corps and prepared to depart México, I refused to say goodbye to a people, a country, even buildings we had come to love – love in the purest sense of the word. Yes, even love for buildings and not just historic, beautiful, ancient churches and cathedrals because there are billions of them in México. That's a recently intensely researched fact – maybe trillions (Rush Bimbo, 2005, *God Got Greedy in México*). They range in size from the tiny pueblo classic-style stone or adobe missions to big city cathedrals, literally the size of Manhattan – another solidly researched fact right out of Bimbo's classic. I love them all, and I'm not even Catholic.

I also loved the diversity of building types in México largely because they are diverse in color, but not necessarily so much in structure, like the example of San Joaquin, Sierra Gorda. Like much of Latin America, stores and homes often run the entire spectrum of color, both the exterior and interior. These are bright colors, with what appears to be no color coordination like we see in almost every, certainly new, neighborhood in the United States. For example, the covenants in our subdivision require we paint using only earth tones. Maybe this explains why depression and cabin fever, or seasonal affective disorder (SAD) are so common at higher latitudes. Seattle and Fairbanks could take a few lessons from México.

Any Street, United States

San Joaquin, Sierra Gorda

Let me tell you more about La Casita, which totally stole my heart. In addition to the small cramped bathroom, just about everything else was in miniature. We could clean the entire place in one hour. As we were moving our minimalist belongings in to La Casita, the owner swung by with a "new" flat screen TV. Well, the screen was flat but it had one massive cathode ray tube backing it up, and it sat on a cart. TV trays did not come with it. The couch for viewing was unquestionably the most uncomfortable couch in which I've ever sat, but it kept you awake. The walls were dark blue, dark green and lime green.

Outside, we had one lemon tree and one lime tree in the front patio and an old washer, clothesline and squawking parrots on the back patio. Directly behind us was a seminary, so we had to watch our parties carefully. I could get on the flat roof by ladder and watch the migratory habits of the evening birds while drinking straight shots of tequila or collecting limes and lemons. Very deluxe.

I'll be damned if I am permanently saying *adios* to that little place where we just spent over three uncomplicated, fantastic years of our lives. To augment the simplicity, we had no car sitting at the curb needing our care and feeding. Apparently, La Casita didn't want to say goodbye to us either, and she (females tend to be more emotional, correct?) demonstrated her displeasure just after we moved out and into a grand home in the UNESCO World Heritage Site center of Querétaro.

Peace Corps Director's Hacienda

We temporarily moved into the several-hundred-year-old hacienda owned by our first Peace Corps director and his wife, loaned to us while they were visiting the United States. I don't want to dwell on the size of the hacienda, but you need some perspective. La Casita would fit comfortably into their kitchen. Eagles nested at one end of the football field-length patio garden. I could barely see their nest, even with binoculars. They preyed on wildlife (e.g., rabbits, armadillos, deer and feral dogs) living on the premises. Anyway, the new tenants of our beloved La Casita, a wonderful Peace Corps couple, just like us, had been cavorting on the beach during the transition week we moved. When they came back to their new home, they encountered the following scene (direct quote from their email):

"Hi, Sonya and David. Hope you are doing well and enjoying time at the director's house. We got back from our trip last night and walked into a disaster area at our new casa. Sometime last week the whole ceiling in the kitchen caved in. They have been working to repair it, but the main level of the house is all torn up. The kitchen cabinets had to be removed and are in the living room. All the kitchen dishes, pots, microwave, etc. are piled in the main bedroom. There is a thick layer of concrete dust on every surface. There is a huge pile of old concrete out on the street by the curb. They have fashioned a new ceiling of concrete, and it is drying now. We were able to sleep in the upstairs room, but it will be some time before the house is very livable again. I don't know if you heard about it, but I wanted to let you know. You got out just in time!"

I responded immediately:

"Honestly, it saddens me to hear your story, but at the same time I have to laugh. In México, that is the ONLY alternative – to laugh. Cry simultaneously if you have to, but never get mad. If you can do that under circumstances like you just described, I guarantee you will love this country. I can't say that I have always followed my own advice. I promise you that when all the dust settles (pun intended) you will be extremely happy in La Casita. I refuse to get maudlin, but we are taking home with us some great, great memories, for many of which that little house was center stage. Our Méxican experience was made that much richer because we truly loved living there."

My question: is there a take-home-to-the-United States message buried somewhere in this story? Absolutely, at least that was my intention. But my "take homes" are usually not readily obvious on the first or maybe even the fourth reading. Thus, I must turn to Chicken Little for help, who might have conceivably said to the small, saddened cement structure, "Yes, La Casita, your ceiling may have fallen when Los Gringos Greegors left, but it was not the sky. They will return." And we *will* be back to visit La Casita, Querétaro, and México. When we do, we will definitely go by and visit her partly because our landlords became our good friends and still live in the adjoining house. But when we go back to the little house, we'll also be there for the friends, the city and the country that gave us so much. Furthermore, we still won't tolerate no stinkin' despedidas, but only fiestas. And, as long as we are able and not too feeble, we will keep returning. Why? Because La Casita *is* México. It is symbolic of our almost four year Mexican experience. That tiny apartment represents hundreds of experiences, blended into a collage of brilliant colors, fiestas, diversity and love. Diversity and love of individuals, cultures, music, food, and yes, even buildings.

~~~~~~~~~~~

Note from the author:
If you enjoyed reading this novel, please consider leaving a review on Amazon and/or Goodreads. Reviews really help encourage more readers (and make the author rich!). Thank you for reading *Going to México*!

davegreegor.com

Acknowledgements

After returning to the United States after four years of Peace Corps service, the people, the culture and the environments of México continued to assault my mind, fueling a strong desire to publish the stories I'd written during our time in México. The result was *Going to Mexico*. Reworking each story wasn't difficult because it allowed me to relive those incredible moments. I am eternally grateful to communities like Chitejé de Garabato and Chitejé de la Cruz where my wife, Sonya, and I began and ended our volunteer work, to the Peace Corps México staff, to Peace Corps Group 5, my group and the best ever, to the SEMARNAT employees who tolerated me, to my editor Kathy, to Craig for his formatting wisdom, to Debora for designing the jacket and for help formatting, and to those who willing gave testimonials for the back cover – Byron, Janet and Ron.

Sonya helped immeasurably with the editing and story selection as well as playing a key role in many of the stories. She has incredible patience not only for hanging with me for 44 years, including almost a decade in which she watched this project dribble along like a deflated basketball. For those reasons and many more, everyone, including me, agrees that she is the real Superwoman.

Peace Corps Group 5 in Colima National Park

ABOUT THE AUTHOR

David H. Greegor is a retired university professor with a doctorate in Ecology. He lived in Querétaro, México for four years as a Peace Corps volunteer. During those years he helped the Mexican federal environmental agency address environmental problems and solutions in central México's poor villages. Research and recreation have taken him to Central and South America, New Zealand and Antarctica, where he has a mountain named in his honor. He has written many editorials and articles combining humor with environmental issues. David lives in Boise, Idaho with his harmonicas and his wife, Sonya.

davegreegor.com

Made in the USA
Columbia, SC
26 August 2017